W9-ANT-774

2009 01 29

WEB SITE
PUBLIC RELATIONS

WEB SITE PUBLIC RELATIONS

How Corporations Build and Maintain Relationships Online

Mihaela Vorvoreanu

CAMBRIA PRESS

AMHERST, NEW YORK

Requests for permission should be directed to:
permissions@cambriapress.com, or mailed to:
Cambria Press
20 Northpointe Parkway, Suite 188
Amherst, NY 14228

Library of Congress Cataloging-in-Publication Data

Vorvoreanu, Mihaela.
    Web site public relations : how corporations build and maintain relationships online / Mihaela Vorvoreanu.
        p. cm.
    Includes bibliographical references and index.
    ISBN 978-1-60497-528-4 (alk. paper)
    1. Internet in public relations. 2. Corporations—Public relations. I. Title.

    HD59.V67 2008
    659.20285'4678—dc22

2008012537

TABLE OF CONTENTS

LIST OF TABLES

List of Tables

FOREWORD

It is no secret that Web sites have emerged as a massively popular and important tool in public relations, marketing, organizational communication, political campaigns, and a host of other fields. Thus, it is not surprising that many people view Web sites as a cutting-edge area for both practice and research. What is surprising is the tiny percentage of Web site research that reflects the latest thinking in research and practice. Indeed, it is probably fair to say that research about the *newest and latest* communication technologies is typically conducted either atheoretically or using only the *oldest* conceptual designs and methodologies— usually simple linear sender and message-centered approaches. Atheoretical Web site research often involves mere descriptive content analyses of Web pages, for example, what percent have video clips on their front page. A simple linear approach might seek to discover the "magic bullet" a Web page could use to make visitors read its content or buy a product (or candidate) that is being promoted. Since such magic bullets do not exist in Web page design any more than they do in public relations or health communication, that quest is certain to be a long one.

The result of using these old approaches has been that research on homepages largely has been unable to address the most central question in all modern marketing and public relations research and practice: How can organizations build and maintain *relationships* with their publics/customers? This relational focus has characterized marketing research and practice since at least the early 1980s and public relations since the late 1980s, yet Web page design and use has, on the whole, failed to adopt it. Vorvoreanu's *Web Site Public Relations* steps in to fill this void and help move Web site research and use toward a more professional and theoretic foundation.

This book is an original and rigorous attempt to build a model of the experience of visiting Web sites that places the visitor—rather than the sponsor or Web page—at the center of the experience. Although it is one of the first such attempts, this book's rigor, theoretic foundation, and genuine insightfulness suggest that it will stand the test of time and may well become one of the most influential works in visitor-centered research on Web sites and the Internet. As such, the findings reported here will be of interest to those who use the Internet, whether for personal or commercial purposes, as well as those seeking to study the social and behavioral effects of the Internet, including those seeking to study its effects on children and adolescents.

Web Site Public Relations focuses attention on the cognitions, attitudes, and behaviors visitors exhibit while visiting Web sites. The conceptual framework that results, as well as the research protocol Vorvoreanu develops and explains, illustrates, and explains the structure and anatomy of visitors' experiences on Web sites along two major dimensions: time and space. The time dimension addresses the sequence of events a visitor goes through on a Web site, while the spatial dimension addresses where a visitor goes while on a Web site and by what routes.

Vorvoreanu's framework and protocol will provide those concerned with the influence Web sites may be having on youth with the theoretic and procedural tools they need to approach the issue in new and, hopefully, fruitful ways. Alternatively, those concerned with how publics relate to a marketing Web site compared to their competitors' marketing site will also have new tools to use. Even scholars and homeland security experts seeking to understand how terrorist Web sites build relationships with potential terrorists will have a new and more sophisticated tool for their work.

The advent of what has come to be called Web 2.0 makes Vorvoreanu's work even more important than it would have been when older Web technologies dominated because Web 2.0 includes such things as user-powered content sites, and the like. A way to understand how visitors experience such Web sites is critical to learning how to harness their new potential.

This book, then, will be invaluable for teachers and practitioners who find old-fashioned sender or message-centered approaches to homepages wanting. Those who just want to better understand their own Internet experience may find this well-written book even more valuable, however, and a pleasure to read.

Carl Botan, PhD
Professor and Director
PhD Program in Health and Strategic Communication
George Mason University

PREFACE

This research was completed in July 2004 and its focus was online relationship building between organizations and their publics. The research produced a conceptual framework of the relationship building online experience and an associated research protocol for analyzing this experience. Besides the framework and research protocol, the main contribution this research made to the public relations literature is the theory-based, experience-centered approach to studying online relationship building. The experience-centered approach is a much needed complement to message-focused, exploratory, and often atheoretical existing literature.

Unfortunately, not much has changed in public relations Web site research since the summer of 2004. Exploration of Web site content and features is still the dominant paradigm of public relations Web site research, and content analysis is still the dominant methodology. The fundamental question driving public relations Web site research has remained atheoretical and exploratory, and is often worded as: How do...(certain kinds of organizations) use their Web sites? A welcome trend is that the focus of inquiry has expanded beyond U.S. organizations. For example, Alfonso and Valbuena Miguel (2006) examined the content and features of online press rooms of 120 companies from Denmark, France, Germany, Norway, Singapore, Spain, the United Kingdom, and the United States. Ayish (2005) and Kirat (2007) looked at the use of Web sites by organizations in the United Arab Emirates. Like most other content analyses, these studies created inventories of the types of content available on the Web sites (number of press releases, backgrounders, videos, etc.) and of certain Web site features (navigation path, interactivity, feedback, etc.).

One remarkable study that breaks away from the exploratory content analytic genre is Bennett's (2005) analysis of charity Web sites. Bennett drew upon marketing research in atmospherics, defined as the ambiance of a place, and their effect on consumer emotions and behavior. Bennett applied the concept of atmospherics to charity Web sites, and explored the effect of Web site features and design on consumer emotions, telepresence, approach/avoidance behavior, and conative responses. Bennett integrated these variables into a parsimonious model that predicts approach/avoidance behavior and conative responses. Bennett's study addresses a very important aspect of the Web site experience, namely the emotions that arise in response to the ambience, or atmosphere, created by Web site content and design. Future research could integrate atmospherics into the conceptual framework of the public relations Web site experience proposed in this book.

Developments in scholarly research happen at a much slower pace than developments in technology and public relations practice. The slow development of scholarly research is by no means an indicator of stagnation of Internet technologies. On the contrary, since the completion of this research, Web technologies have moved to a different stage altogether. This different stage is Web 2.0.

Although there is still debate over the exact definition of Web 2.0, the concept is associated with a new generation of Web applications characterized by rich, data-driven Web sites, user-powered content, and social networking (O'Reilly, 2005). Technologies such as blogs, RSS feeds, social networking sites (Facebook, MySpace, LinkedIn, etc.), user-powered content sites (digg.com, del.icio.us, reddit, YouTube, flickr, wikis), and virtual worlds (such as Second Life) are all examples of Web 2.0 applications. Public relations practitioners are still exploring the potentials and pitfalls of such technologies for online relationship building. Some of these technologies, such as blogs and RSS feeds, are already used in public relations. Others are still the domain of very early adopters only. Practice-oriented articles about these Web 2.0 technologies have been published in trade publications such as *PRSA Tactics*, but not in scholarly journals. The use of blogs for corporate public relations is the topic of a new book, *Strategies and Tools for Corporate Blogging*, written by a public relations practitioner (Cass, 2007). The early adopters have just started thinking about the implications of Web 2.0 technologies for public relations. Many other public relations practitioners and scholars are yet unaware of the existence of some of these technologies. It is to be expected, however, that the next big wave of public relations scholarly research will focus on Web 2.0 technologies.

The framework of the public relations Web site experience and the Web site experience analysis research protocol proposed

in this research are still valid and novel concepts, highly appli-
cable to the study of public relations Web sites. It is too early to
tell whether the framework or research protocol can be useful for
the study of Web 2.0 public relations, mainly because Web 2.0
public relations is in the early infancy stage. It is highly probable, however, that the experience-centered approach will provide a valuable theoretical foundation for the examination of
these new media and their uses in public relations.

REFERENCES

Alfonso, G.-H., & Valbuena Miguel, R. (2006). Trends in online media relations: Web-based corporate press rooms in leading international companies. *Public Relations Review, 32*(3), 267–275.

Ayish, M. I. (2005). Virtual public relations in the United Arab Emirates: A case study of 20 UAE's organizations' use of the Internet. *Public Relations Review, 31*(3), 381–388.

Bennett, R. (2005). Antecedents and consequences of Website atmosphere in online charity fundraising situations. *Journal of Website Promotion, 1*(1), 131–152.

Cass, J. (2007). *Strategies and tools for corporate blogging.* Oxford, U.K.: Elsevier.

Kirat, M. (2007). Promoting online media relations: Public relations departments' use of the Internet in the UAE. *Public Relations Review, 33*(2), 166–174.

O'Reilly, T. (2005). *What is Web 2.0: Design patterns and business models for the next generation of software.* Retrieved June 2007 from http://www.oreillynet.com.

EXECUTIVE SUMMARY

INTRODUCTION

Since the 1980s, Web sites have emerged as a major communication medium between organizations and their publics. As a public relations tool, Web sites have several attractive characteristics: cost-effectiveness, interactivity, multimedia capability, wide reach, and last but not least, direct access to the public, or the ability to bypass mass media gatekeeping. It comes as no surprise, then, that organizations big and small have taken advantage of this new communication environment to create virtual store fronts for their online publics. There is wide agreement among both practitioners and scholars that Web sites are important public relations media. However, online public relations practice has advanced faster than research and scholarship; so although Web sites are widely used in public relations, they are not thoroughly understood. Therefore, the fundamental question driving this research is how Web sites can accomplish the public relations purpose of building and maintaining relationships with stakeholders. Acknowledgment of the rapidly-changing nature of Internet communication and of the complexity of public relations leads to the development of a conceptual framework and associated research protocol—Web site experience analysis—that can be employed to answer this fundamental question for different types of Web sites, organizations, publics, and situations.

EXISTING LITERATURE

The development of the present framework of the public relations Web site experience and the associated research protocol is grounded in a thorough review of four areas of literature: Internet communication, Web site design, communication Web site research, and organization-public relationship building.

To understand the Internet as a communication environment, this research looked into foundational ideas from the history of the Internet and World Wide Web. Ideals such as sharing of resources, free and open access, and lack of central control are manifested in the technologies at the core of the Internet and influence the nature of online communication.

The Web site design literature focused on user experience and user-centered design informs this research and provides a much needed complement to the message-centered approach of previous public relations Web site studies. Also, the Web site design literature provides insight into the structural components of Web sites, which can be fine-tuned to provide an improved user experience.

Previous communication research that has focused on organizational, political, and personal Web sites is reviewed in order to isolate and understand the theoretical frameworks and research methodologies used in the scholarly inquiry of Web sites. The overwhelming majority of communication studies uses an exploratory, atheoretical approach to Web site research, and employs content analysis to survey the various message features of Web sites. The present research fills a gap in existing communication literature because it provides a conceptual, theory-based approach to the study of Web sites, and a research protocol that examines the Web site visitor's experience, as opposed to the Web site message.

Relationship building between organizations and their public is the fourth and last major area of literature that informs this research. Building and maintaining positive, long-lasting, mutually-beneficial relationships between organizations and their publics is the purpose of public relations, as agreed upon by communication researchers of various theoretical orientations. Public relations scholarship about relationship building and maintenance, and especially about dimensions of organization-public relationships, significantly contributes to the conceptual foundation of this research.

A CONCEPTUAL FRAMEWORK OF THE PUBLIC RELATIONS WEB SITE EXPERIENCE

This research study argues for an experience-centered approach to the study of public relations Web sites. An experience-centered approach is a useful complement to the message focus of previous content-analytic research. Instead of examining message content and message strategies, the experience approach examines public members' cognitions, attitudes and online behaviors as they occur during the interaction with an organization's Web site.

A conceptual framework of the public relations Web site experience is proposed. The framework illustrates the structure and anatomy of the experience of visiting a public relations

Web site. The two major dimensions of the Web site experience framework are time and space. The temporal dimension is defined as the sequence of behaviors, cognitions, and emotions users experience in time, as they visit a Web site. The spatial dimension is defined as the virtual space of the Web site itself. The two dimensions are further broken down into structural elements such as phases and modules.

The Web site experience itself is defined as the activation of interconnections between the spatial and temporal dimensions. These interconnections will differ among publics and even among individuals.

A NEW RESEARCH PROTOCOL: WEB SITE EXPERIENCE ANALYSIS

Web site experience analysis is proposed as a new research protocol that can be employed to analyze the public relations Web site experience. The construction of this new research protocol is derived from the conceptual framework of the Web site experience and draws upon usability research and prominence-interpretation theory. Web site experience analysis requires a sample of an organization's public to visit the organization's Web site and to answer a questionnaire about the online experience. To illustrate how this new research protocol can be used and what types of insights it can produce, Web site experience analysis was conducted with a sample of 45 undergraduate students on nine organizational Web sites.

WEB SITE EXPERIENCE ANALYSIS FINDINGS AND IMPLICATIONS

The results of the pilot Web site experience analysis indicated what specific elements of the Web site virtual space are associated by this specific public with relationship-building efforts, and how they are interpreted. The data demonstrate that Web site experience analysis can be a very useful tool for both public relations practitioners and scholars.

Used in public relations practice, Web site experience analysis can help practitioners fine-tune aspects of the organization's Web site to engineer an experience conducive to building and maintaining positive relationships with stakeholders. For public relations scholarly research, Web site experience analysis can provide in-depth insights into the complex phenomenon of building relationships between organizations and publics. Furthermore, the Web site experience analysis research protocol can be easily modified to suit other kinds of communication inquiry that might not be focused on relationship building, such as risk or health communication.

This research makes important contributions to both public relations scholarship and practice. The conceptual framework of the public relations Web site experience and the experience-centered approach to public relations are this study's most significant contributions to public relations scholarship. The new research protocol, Web site experience analysis, contributes to both scholarship and practice. Public relations practitioners in particular are likely to find this research protocol a convenient and inexpensive way to gain insights into their publics' online public relations experiences.

ACKNOWLEDGMENTS

This research project has benefited tremendously from Dr. Carl Botan's direction, support, and guidance through the sometimes murky processes of academia. Thank you, Carl. Your faith in me has enabled me to try things I had no idea I could do.

I would like to thank my husband, Krishna Madhavan, and my family in Romania and India. Their unconditional love and support is my stable ground, the foundation for everything that I am and do.

The staff at Cambria Press has been a pleasure to work with. Thank you for your patient and kind assistance.

WEB SITE
PUBLIC RELATIONS

CHAPTER 1

INTRODUCTION AND UNDERLYING ASSUMPTIONS

"Cogito, ergo sum," said Descartes, claiming the philosophical proof of human existence in the act of thinking. "I have a Web site, therefore I am" might very well be the translation of Descartes' statement from 17th-century philosophy into 21st-century public relations. A World Wide Web presence has become as common and necessary as being listed in the telephone book. "The Internet is like a store front for world business. If you're not there, you're not even close to doing business this day and age," said a public relations practitioner (White & Raman, 2000). Web sites have become necessary public relations tools. The ubiquitous presence of public relations Web sites proves that organizations understand this need and attempt to meet it. Consequently, Web sites have also become an important topic for public relations research. Theory, however, lags behind practice in the area of public relations Web sites. This research project intends to address the need to develop theory by proposing a framework of the public relations Web site experience.

Public relations scholars agree that the purpose of public relations is to build positive, mutually beneficial relationships between organizations and stakeholders (Botan, 1992; Broom, Casey, & Ritchey, 1997, 2000; J. E. Grunig & Huang, 2000; Hallahan, 2003; Heath, 2000; Kent & Taylor, 1998; Ledingham, 2003; Ledingham & Bruning, 1998). Organizations engage in a variety of relationship-building communication strategies and behaviors. One important tool for relationship building and maintenance is the organizational Web site. Web sites have many characteristics that make them attractive for public relations (Esrock & Leichty, 1998). One of the main advantages is that the gatekeeping function of mass media does not operate on the World Wide Web—organizations are free to make public any information they desire, without having to pass through the selective process of the mass media. Another advantage of Web sites is that they can have built-in interactive features that facilitate two-way communication. Through the use of feedback features, an organization can easily collect information, monitor public opinion, and get input from its publics. Finally, Web sites tend to serve active audiences that seek information and are already motivated to listen to what the organization has to say (Esrock & Leichty). Kent and Taylor maintain that the WWW provides organizations the opportunity to move beyond monologue and create dialogic relationships with their publics.

It is no surprise then, that organizations use Web sites for public relations purposes to build and maintain relationships with their stakeholders. By virtue of being rich and dynamic communication environments, Web sites provide their visitors with complex experiences. Multiple aspects of these experiences, such as the navigation, graphic design, or interactivity of a Web site have the potential to influence Web site visitors' perceptions. The fundamental questions guiding this study are: What is the nature of a public relations Web site experience? How is organization-public relationship-building work performed on Web sites? What roles do various aspects of Web site construction play in the relationship building/maintenance experience?

The project rests on the premises that Web sites constitute a major communication force in today's society; and that as complex communication environments, they offer new and multiple possibilities for expression, persuasion, and dialogue. The project sets out to inquire what these possibilities are and how they work together to shape the public relations experience of Web users. The aim of the project is to propose a conceptual framework of the public relations Web site experience that can be used to understand, analyze, and improve this experience.

The remainder of this chapter lays the foundation for this project. First, I define the context and focus of this research and discuss the views and assumptions underlying it. Then, I clarify the project's goals and provide an overview of subsequent chapters.

THE WORLD WIDE WEB VERSUS THE INTERNET

The Internet and the World Wide Web are terms often, but incorrectly, used interchangeably. A distinction between the two is necessary in order to understand the object of this study and its boundaries.

The technology that makes computer communication and data sharing possible is the Internet. The Internet is a global network of computer networks that supports many types of communication, such as e-mail, file transfers, instant messaging, and the World Wide Web. Tim Berners-Lee, the creator of the World Wide Web, puts it very simply when he explains that at its core the Internet is made up of computers and cables that connect them (Berners-Lee, 2002). The World Wide Web is one of many communication protocols that run on the Internet. It is a way of making information available on the Internet in the form of interlinked texts, images, sounds, video clips, and so forth (Berners-Lee, 2002).

Of all the forms of communication supported on the Internet, this project focuses on Web sites, and more specifically, on corporate public relations Web sites. The next section clarifies the focus of this research.

PROJECT FOCUS

The focus of this research is limited to U.S. business corporations' Web sites, which are studied from a public relations perspective. To some extent, the terms "public relations Web site" and "relationship-building Web site" are intrinsically redundant, because it can be argued that all Web sites contribute to building some kind of relationship with one public or another. Most, if not all, Web sites can be assumed to play somewhat of a public relations role, whether intended or not. This redundancy notwithstanding, the two terms are used throughout this study to emphasize the focus on planned, strategic efforts undertaken by organizations to create Web site experiences that build and maintain relationships with various publics. When examining Web sites, this research focuses on how the various elements of Web site content and design create an online experience conducive to initiating and maintaining relationships with site visitors.

Because most, if not all, Web sites build some kind of relationship with some kind of public, it becomes very difficult to distinguish between public relations and nonpublic relations Web sites. Instead of dwelling on this distinction, it might be more productive to conceptualize public relations as a function or purpose of Web sites. Various organizations' and even countries' so-called online headquarters (Web sites that provide general information about an organization or country, usually identified by the use of the organization's name in the URLs, such as www.ge.com, www.redcross.org, or www.poland.com) have a very strong public relations function and have been studied before from a public relations perspective (Brunn & Cottle, 1997; Durham, 2000; Esrock & Leichty, 1998, 1999, 2000; Gustavsen & Tilley, 2003; Jackson & Purcell, 1997; Kent, Taylor, & White, 2003; Marken, 2002; Taylor, Kent, & White, 2001). The phrase "public relations Web sites" is used throughout this study as shorthand, to refer to Web sites with a very strong public relations function. Although various types of organizations, and even nations and governments, create Web sites with strong public relations functions, the scope of this research is limited to corporate Web sites authored by U.S. business corporations.

Two main reasons account for limiting the project's scope to U.S. corporate Web sites. First, corporations are innovators and Web content pioneers (O'Leary, 2002). They have the resources and the motivation to invest in their Web sites and to implement the newest technologies and online communication strategies. U.S. corporations spend millions of dollars a year to maintain their Web sites (Jupiter Media Metrix, 2002) and can afford to innovate and set trends that other types of organizations follow. Second, most existing public relations research focuses on corporate Web sites, and this project aims to build upon this body of research.

The major trend in corporate Web site design is the focus on user experience. This research project adopts the same point of view, and articulates an experience-oriented theoretical perspective that underlies the study. This approach is described next.

THE WEB SITE EXPERIENCE

The terms "Web site experience" and "user experience" have recently emerged at the forefront of Web design and programming literature. Providing a positive user experience is the major guiding principle in Web site design (Berry, 2000; Hurst & Gellady, 1999; IBM, 2003a; Nielsen, 1997; Nielsen & Norman, 2000; Shedroff, 2001). Despite this focus on building a positive user experience on Web sites, the literature lacks a rigorous definition of the concept itself. Paul (2000) defined Web site experience loosely as the user's overall satisfaction with the site. This definition is problematic because it does not address the experience itself, only a set of attitudes and opinions related to the Web site visit. In lieu of a definition, some authors mention characteristics of the Web user experience and factors that contribute to positive experiences: quick, easy, and predictable operation of the site, good navigation, secure transactions, ease of learning, efficiency of use, memorability, fresh content, personalization, and so forth (Hurst & Gellady; Nielsen; Nielsen & Norman; Paul). The literature suggests that the subjective experience of Web users is largely dependent upon characteristics of the Web site, and that the user experience can be improved by careful design (Shedroff, 2001), but fails to provide a conceptually clear or comprehensive definition of the Web site experience, or an explanation of how Web site characteristics interact to create it.

Three conclusions can be drawn from the literature about the Web user experience: (1) it lacks both a rigorous definition and insight from theory-driven research; (2) it combines subjective perceptions with Web site characteristics; and (3) it can be influenced by altering the Web site design. Theory-driven research on the Web user experience is needed to address the conceptual and theoretical shortcomings of the literature and to provide more systematic, theory-based insights and recommendations for improving and customizing the Web site experience. Such research has value for both public relations scholarship and practice, because there is an overwhelming sense among industry specialists that the Web site experience is of major importance for the conduct of business and public relations online.

The costs of poor user experiences are great, say industry specialists, because users abandon sites they are frustrated with. In the case of e-commerce sites, this results in a direct loss of money (Hurst & Gellady, 1999). On the other hand, a positive Web user experience is believed to hold the key to increased sales, return visits, and good relationships with site visitors (Goldie, 2003; Hurst & Gellady, 1999; IBM, 2003b; Nielsen, 1997; Nielsen & Norman, 2000; Paul, 2000; Souza, Manning, Sonderegger, Roshan, & Dorsey, 2001).

Thinking of Web sites as experiences can be more than a Web design trend. This project takes the emphasis on Web site user experience one step further and articulates theoretical and methodological implications of examining Web sites as experiences as opposed to texts.

Experience Versus Text
What does it mean to think of Web sites as experiences, not as texts? Bringing up the notion of text opens a vast discussion about the meaning of text as a rhetorical artifact. The meaning of text has changed over time and has expanded from written

or spoken verbal discourse to include other, nonverbal, types of expression such as buildings (Berman, 1999), monuments (Blair, Jeppeson, & Pucci Jr., 1995; Foss, 1986) or cartoons (Bostdorff, 1987; Edwards & Winkler, 1997). Digital multimedia messages that include both verbal and nonverbal discourse, such as Web sites, could easily be considered texts and have been the subject of rhetorical and textual analyses (Brunn & Cottle, 1997; Fursich & Robins, 2002, 2004; Hernon, 1998; Jackson & Purcell, 1997; McKeown & Plowman, 1999; Mitra, 1997; Purcell & Kodras, 2001; Tian, 2006; Zhang & Benoit, 2004).

The lack of a rigorous definition of the concept of Web site experience makes it difficult to identify clear boundaries between experiences and texts. There are at least two important characteristics, however, that set experiences apart from texts: interactivity and control. Texts have audiences; experiences have participants (Aarseth, 1997; S. Johnson, 1997; Landow, 1997; Nelson, 1992; Shedroff, 2001). Experience participants interact with the artifact and have greater control than text audiences over the nature and pace of this interaction.

Moreover, associated with the notion of text is the connotation that the researcher analyzes the rhetorical artifact, not the audience's experience of interacting with and using this artifact. This project advocates a research perspective that focuses on the Web site user's experience rather than the structural and content features of the Web site. The argument has been made before, in favor of analyzing the experience of using the text rather than the text itself (Fish, 1980). Fish, the founder of reader-response theory in literary criticism, argued that textual analysis is grounded in the mistaken assumption that there is meaning in the text, a meaning that awaits discovery. Following the arguments of the linguistic turn and social constructionism, he argued that meaning is not in the text: It is created interactively in the process of reading, which is entirely interpretation. Therefore, instead of analyzing formal features of literary texts, Fish advocated focusing on the reader's interpretation experience, as it unfolds in time.

The same philosophy of communication applies to Web sites. The Web site, taken as a text, is not a repository of meaning waiting to be extracted by Web site visitors. Meaning is created in the process of interaction between the visitor and the Web site. In this process, the pace and nature of the experience, along with words and images on screen, are subject to interpretation and therefore elements of meaning making. If we are to understand the role Web sites play in public relations, we have to look not only at Web site characteristics, but also at people's experiences with those Web sites and the meanings that emerge from these experiences.

In addition to these theoretical reasons, there is a practical reason why it is preferable to examine the Web site experience and not the Web site alone. In the case of Web site analysis, it is hard to analyze the text (Web site), because the text is fluid and potentially varies with each visitor (Aarseth, 1997; Landow, 1994; McMillan, 2000; Slatin, 1991). At a very concrete level, the Web site text is created by each visitor through the choice of links and pages to view. If the text varies with each visit, then what is the text that should be analyzed? And by analyzing the text alone, don't researchers miss out on the significance of the choices Web site users make?

The risks of adopting an interpretive, experience-focused perspective are endless relativism and subjectivism. If text and interpretation vary with each Web site visitor, one could argue that there are no similarities among different Web site visits or across Web site visitors. Therefore, experiences should be studied one at a time, without any hope or possibility for generalization. Fish (1980, 2001) addressed this objection and counters it with the notion of interpretive communities. Interpretive communities, he stated, are composed of people who share a set of interpretive strategies. These interpretive strategies emerge from shared assumptions, a common language, a collective body of knowledge, and so forth. People who belong to the same interpretive community tend to interpret texts in similar ways and to create similar meanings. This way, generalization becomes possible, but one should be cautious generalizing beyond the boundaries of an interpretive community. An interpretive community, engrossed in its own worldview, might not accept or even see the meaning taken for granted in another community.

Fish's concept of interpretive communities is consistent with the social constructionist epistemology in communication theory, which claims that meanings are culturally constructed, and therefore local, and warns against broad generalizations. The concept of interpretive communities (Fish, 1980, 2001) is not foreign to public relations either, where it finds a close correspondent in the notion of publics. An organization's public shares a set of assumptions, interpretations and values (Botan & Soto, 1998), interests (Dewey, 1927), cognitions and behaviors (J. E. Grunig & Hunt, 1984) which place its members in the same interpretive community (Vasquez, 1993) or zone of meaning (Heath, 1993). Publics interact with and interpret organizational discourse, not literary texts, but the same dynamics of an interpretive community constructing meaning from a text apply. Thus, reader-response theory and public relations share important basic assumptions that make it possible to approach public relations Web sites from an experience-centered perspective. The experience-centered perspective focuses on the public's experience and interpretation of Web sites. The next section discusses the implications of adopting this perspective.

Implications of an Experience-Centered Perspective

A focus on the Web site experience has important implications for communication research. If the object of analysis is not the text, as it exists independent of audiences, but the lived experience of using and interacting with a Web site, it becomes essential to understand the participants and the nature of their experiences. Methodologically, it follows that textual or content analysis should be replaced with the observation and analysis of people's experiences using Web sites and the meanings they create in the process. Such a research methodology that uses both quantitative and qualitative data to tap into Web site users' experiences and interpretations, is developed and used in this research project, as explained in chapter 4.

Ignoring the Web site user can lead to misleading conclusions in Web site analysis. For example, a researcher analyzing online media rooms used the number of content categories available in each media room as a measure of media room elaboration (Callison, 2003). Media room elaboration was considered a positive aspect in this study and provided a basis for making inferences about the overall quality of online media rooms. The problem with this operationalization is that it completely ignores the Web site user. The overall elaboration and quality of a media room are determined not only by the quantity of available content but also by the means of navigating and accessing this content. The latter aspect was completely ignored in Callison's study, illustrating a major drawback of content analysis as a method for studying Web sites.

So far, this chapter has explained the theoretical perspectives that inform this research—a relationship-focused public relations perspective and an experience-centered approach to Web sites—as well as the methodological implications of adopting these perspectives. The remainder of this chapter discusses corporate Web sites and their importance in today's society, and specifies this project's goals.

WEB SITES: MAJOR COMMUNICATION FORCE IN CONTEMPORARY WESTERN SOCIETY

Online user behavior data show that the number of Web sites is massive, and that people make intense and frequent use of them. The Web has become, at least in Western society, a major source of information. People look to the Web for information they use to make crucial decisions. It is important to establish what role Web sites in general and corporate Web sites in particular play in today's society. If Web sites are not a major communication force, it would be hard to justify investing effort and time studying them. This section provides a summary of data about Web usage in North America, and when available, throughout the world. The data shows that Web sites play important roles in many aspects of everyday life.

How Many Online?
Reports from the U.S. Department of Commerce based on U.S. Census data show that more than half of the U.S. population is online (U.S. Department of Commerce, 2002, 2004). In September 2001, 54% of Americans or 143 million people were online (U.S. Department of Commerce, 2002). By September 2003, this percentage grew to 58.7% (U.S. Department of Commerce, 2004). This number is growing, according to the 2002 report, by 2 million new users every month. The same report shows that the growth rate of Internet connectivity is large for

all income groups. Actually, the largest annual growth rate, of 25%, is encountered among the lowest income bracket (under $15,000 per year). At the end of 2002, there were an estimated 580 million people online worldwide, of which 168.6 million Americans (Nielsen//NetRatings, 2003), and about a hundred million Web sites worldwide (Nielsen, 2000a). In 2004 the estimated number of people online worldwide was over 729 million, and the number of Americans online, over 204 million (Global Reach, 2004). Data from 2007 lists over a billion (1,319,872,109) people online worldwide, out of which 211 million live in the United States (Internet World Stats, 2008). These numbers show that Web sites have an enormous potential audience and that the Internet is a major communication medium used by a large number of people all around the world. The great reach of the World Wide Web is an important factor validating the relevance of studying Web sites.

We know that a large number of people have Internet access, but what do they do online? Data show that Americans use the WWW for a wide range of activities. According to the most recent U.S. Department of Commerce report (2004), the most popular use of the Internet is e-mail, followed closely by researching Web sites for product and service information. The next section reviews in more detail the kinds of activities and decisions in which the WWW plays an important role.

Online Activities

Searching for product and service information is an activity 76.5% of American Internet users over the age of 15 reported engaging in (U.S. Department of Commerce, 2004). Online shopping is another major activity among U.S. Internet users. More than 50% of U.S. users made online purchases in 2003 (U.S. Department of Commerce, 2004). In the first quarter of

2002, $9.849 billion was spent online (Cox, 2002). Compare that with $29 billion that was spent online in the 2007 U.S. holiday season (November 1–December 31) (comScore Media Matrix, 2008). Public relations corporate Web sites play an important role in activities related to shopping and searching for information about products and services. Users visit these sites looking for information about products, or about the organization itself and its policies. Research done by Burson-Marsteller and RoperASW (CyberAtlas, 2001) found that online opinion leaders (called "e-fluentials"), who influence an estimated 14 people each, use company Web sites as their main source of information about products and services. Leslie Gaines-Ross, Burson-Marsteller's chief knowledge and research officer, commented on the importance of the company Web site for public relations:

> E-fluentials can be reputation-builders or busters. It's crucial for companies to build trust and value with influential visitors to their Web sites so they can neutralize the negatives and nurture the positives. Company Web sites that provide e-fluentials with straight-forward, easy-to-use information are pivotal in building and enhancing the value of brands, products and services in the public eye. Other consumers count on e-fluentials to be their hunters and gatherers of online information. (CyberAtlas, 2001)

The facts that over 99% of Fortune 500 companies had a Web site as early as 2002 (Russell, 2002) and that almost half a billion dollars was spent on corporate sites in 2001 (Jupiter Media Metrix, 2002) indicate that corporations understand the importance of Web sites.

Web sites also play an important role in information about government and politics. Ninety-seven million Americans reported using government Web sites for finding information or contacting both offices and government officials (Pew Internet and

American Life Project, 2004). Come election time, many U.S. users turn to the Web for political news and information. During the November 2002 midterm elections, 46 million Americans got their political news online and 12% of Net users visited political public relations sites such as those run by the political parties, a candidate, or a campaign (Pew Internet and American Life Project, 2003a, 2003b). These numbers doubled in the 2006 midterm elections (Pew Internet and American Life Project, 2007). Web sites have been used by political candidates for a while now. As early as 1998, more than 63% of political candidates participating in a Congressional Research survey had Web sites and another 21% were planning to launch theirs soon (Moffet, 1998).

Although searching for commercial, political, and other information are major online activities, statistics about other uses of the Web show that Web sites are a part of a wide variety of important decisions. For example, planning and booking travel online is one of the fastest-growing online activities (Pew Internet and American Life Project, 2005). In this context, the public relations function of Web sites sponsored by hotels, resorts, and even nations becomes very important.

Another survey conducted by Pew Internet and American Life (2002) found that Web sites play important roles in a host of U.S. Internet users' life decisions. For example, 14 million Americans reported that the Web played an important role in their choice of car. Almost 9 million people reported that the Web helped them make financial and investment decisions. Corporate Web sites usually have entire sections devoted to financial information and investor relations. More than 11 million Americans relied on the Web to choose a school or college for themselves or a member of their family. Eight million people reported relying on the Internet for finding a job, and another 8 million, for finding a place to live. Almost 14 million U.S. users said the

Web enabled them to help a loved one who had an illness, while more than 4 million reported the Internet helped them cope with a major illness. The growth of these trends has been observed in more recent years, showing that Web sites have become an intrinsic and important part of American life (Pew Internet and American Life Project, 2005).

The data presented here show that a very large number of people rely on the Web for information regarding decisions in many aspects of their lives. Many Web users, in their quest for various kinds of information, make use of corporate Web sites. This makes it important to be able to understand, analyze, and evaluate the public relations experience of visiting corporate Web sites by developing theory about it. This research study sets out to propose and validate a conceptual framework for understanding, analyzing, evaluating, and improving the public relations Web site experience. The study's goals are detailed next.

PROJECT GOALS

The basic question driving this research project inquires about the nature of the experience of visiting a public relations Web site. More specifically, how are organization-public relationships built and maintained online? How does a Web site visitor experience a site that attempts to create and maintain relationships? What aspects of the experience communicate the organization's intention to build a certain kind of relationship? Finding answers to such questions requires the articulation of a theoretical perspective capable of explaining the experience. Therefore, the purpose of this project is to articulate and validate a theoretical framework and associated research protocol for explaining and analyzing the public relations Web site experience. Before articulating such a framework, it is useful to consider the needs and criteria the framework should meet. The following sections discuss criteria for a theory of the public relations Web site experience and the projected utility of such a theory.

Criteria for a Theory of the
Public Relations Web Site Experience

Common criteria for evaluating communication theories are power, heuristic potential, and importance (Botan & Hazleton, 1989; Neuman, 1991; Reinard, 1994; Smith, 1988). In this section, I discuss how these criteria can help shape the framework to be developed in this project.

One of the more important criteria for evaluating theory is power, or the level of the theory. Theories can operate at one or more of three possible levels: description, explanation, and prediction/control. Therefore, a viable theoretical perspective on the experience of visiting a public relations Web site should be able to *describe* this experience: It should provide a vocabulary of concepts useful in talking about the Web site experience, outline the relationships among concepts, and provide an account of how this experience unfolds. Second, the theoretical lens should be able to *explain* the experience of visiting a public relations Web site: It should explain why things happen by exploring causal or at least correlative relationships between concepts. Third, the knowledge gained from the descriptive and explanatory aspects of the theory should provide a basis for intervention. Based on this knowledge, it should be possible to *predict* events given the circumstances, and even to *control* them by manipulating certain conditions. For example, insight gained about the public relations Web site experience should allow one to improve and enhance this experience through theory-driven Web site design.

A second major criterion for assessing the value of a theory is its heuristic potential, or the capacity to stimulate further research. A theoretical perspective on the experience of visiting public relations Web sites could generate further research in at least two foreseeable directions: One direction is to refine and further develop the theory itself by exploring individual concepts and relationships between them in separate studies. Another direction involves attempting to apply the model to other types of Web sites and to adapt it to various contexts.

Third, a theory is judged by its importance, or the relevance of the issues the theory addresses. Data were presented in a previous section establishing the relevance and importance of studying public relations sites. Another aspect of a theory's importance is whether the insight resulting from the theory makes a real difference in the way we understand the phenomena involved. Given the lack of theoretical knowledge about the experience of visiting public relations Web sites, just helping guide inquiry and focus attention on this communication phenomenon might be a meaningful contribution. But a theory of the public relations Web site experience will make a difference in other important ways. The next section explores the projected utility of a theoretical framework of the public relations Web site experience.

Projected Utility of a Theory of the Public Relations Web Site Experience

Research efforts are in part motivated by the conviction that their results will be useful to other people. The present study is partly driven by the belief that a better understanding of the public relations Web site experience would benefit three main audiences: Web users, communication scholars, and public relations practitioners.

As the statistics in the section on the massive role of Web sites in contemporary society show, general Web users are likely to encounter public relations sites frequently. Web users would benefit from being informed and aware consumers of Web sites. Insight gained from a theory of public relations Web sites would help increase online literacy and make users aware of the overt and the subtle persuasive attempts made on such sites. Often, users form a general impression of a Web site but are not always aware what specific Web site aspects contributed to that impression. The difference between self-reported and experimental data about Web site user preferences suggests that people might not be aware of all the Web site aspects that influence their experience (Brinck, Gergle, & Wood, 2002; Nielsen, 2001b). Thus, the information literacy aspect of a theory of the public relations Web site experience would benefit everyday Web site users.

Second, a theory of the experience of visiting public relations Web sites would benefit communication scholars because it would give them a new lens and research protocol they can use to study Web sites, or at the very least it would allow them to perform more informed textual and content analyses. One major challenge in existing textual and content analyses of Web sites is that the artifact is fluid, and possibly changes with every visit (Aarseth, 1997; Landow, 1994; McMillan, 2000; Slatin, 1991). It is very likely that two different people visiting the same Web site at the same point in time will have different experiences, and will not even visit the same pages. If communication scholars understand how people experience Web sites, how they forge a path through information, and how they attend to messages, they will be able to recreate a relatively close approximation of a given public's experience on the Web site and thus be more confident that the object of their analysis is close to the one that the public experiences. For example, analyzing verbal arguments presented in a block of text on a Web site is not necessarily productive, unless researchers take into consideration the placement of that text in the overall site structure, and the visual characteristics of the text such as font size and paragraph length. These characteristics indicate whether that block text is even read by Web site visitors.

Besides enabling researchers to reconstitute the communication artifact a certain public was exposed to, understanding the Web site experience will help communication scholars improve their analyses. A theory of the public relations Web site experience will bring together the various aspects of this experience and the Web site elements that shape it. The awareness of what Web site elements contribute to the user experience, and how they influence it, will allow scholars to include all these elements in their analyses, thus overcoming another major drawback of current Web site studies: truncation. Without a systematic framework to draw attention to the many Web site elements that shape the user experience, scholars sometimes focus their gaze on certain parts of Web sites at the expense of others. One common tendency is to consider the verbal and visual arguments in block text and photographs, and to ignore other Web site aspects, such as navigation menus, structure, or font type, size and color. A theory of the public relations Web site experience that brings together the various persuasive parts of Web sites will enable critics to overcome the truncation limitation and produce complete analyses that do justice to the complexity of the Web site communication environment.

Finally, a theory of the experience of visiting public relations Web sites will benefit public relations practitioners, who would acquire a better understanding of the artifacts they produce and how they are used by publics. Public relations practitioners could use this understanding to enhance and customize the user experience, and to evaluate the extent to which they are achieving their communication goals.

In short, this project's main goal is to create a theoretical framework of the public relations Web site experience. This theoretical framework should function at the three levels of theory: description, explanation, and prediction/control, and it should have heuristic potential. The next section provides an overview of the steps needed in order to formulate and validate a theoretical framework of the experience provided by public relations Web sites.

PROJECT OVERVIEW

To be able to articulate a theoretical framework of the public relations Web site experience, it is first necessary to gain a thorough understanding of the World Wide Web as a communication environment: to understand Web sites, to appreciate the specific characteristics that set them apart from other communication media, and to understand how people use them. Second, it is important to review guidelines and recommendations for constructing good Web sites; and third, to review previous theoretical and methodological perspectives previously used to study the World Wide Web. Finally, the organization-public relationship aspect needs to be better understood. These topics are all discussed in chapter 2, which focuses on previous research that informs this project. The review of previous research is intended to provide a foundation which can be used for constructing a preliminary theoretical framework of the public relations Web site experience. The preliminary model is proposed and described in chapter 3, which introduces two major dimensions of the public relations Web site experience and advances a series of research questions about the relationship between the two dimensions. Chapter 4 introduces a new research protocol: Web site experience analysis, which collects both quantitative and qualitative data to tap into Web site users' interpretations of their online experience. The data collected is presented and discussed in chapter 5. Chapter 6 wraps up the project with concluding thoughts about the utility of the framework, limitations, and opportunities for future research.

CHAPTER 2

BACKGROUND

The literature review part of this project provides an overview of historical, theoretical, and methodological issues related to Web sites and Web site communication. Understanding Web sites, how they work, what they consist of, and how their unique characteristics affect communication is a necessary preliminary step to the development of a framework of the public relations Web site experience. The literature review is divided into four main sections. The first one addresses the World Wide Web as a communication environment. It provides a short history of the major ideas behind the WWW, isolates the core characteristics of Web-based communication, and summarizes existing information about Web site usage. The second section reviews recommendations for effective Web site communication. The purpose of this section is to observe what the constitutive elements of Web site construction and design are and how they can play communicative roles. The third section of the literature review focuses on previous communication research studies of Web sites. These studies can provide useful information about theoretical perspectives and research methods used in the analysis of Web sites. Finally, the fourth section reviews concepts and findings from the public relations literature about building relationships with publics. These bodies of literature provide useful insights to inform the creation of the theoretical framework of the public relations Web site experience.

THE WWW COMMUNICATION ENVIRONMENT

The nature of communication on the WWW is partly shaped by technology and history. In order to fully understand the WWW, it is necessary to know how it was created and how it works. The historical context of the creation of the WWW had quite an impact on the way communication developed in this medium. The technology behind Web sites offers opportunities and imposes limitations on communication, and it has to be understood in order to fully appreciate Web sites as communication media. So this section begins with a short history of the World Wide Web, followed by a brief explanation of what Web sites are and how they work.

A Short History of the WWW

This short secondary account of the history behind the development of the WWW focuses on key ideas and the way they have influenced WWW communication. Different histories of the Internet anchor the story of its development at different starting points: the development of computers and computing machines (Wood & Smith, 2001), or the Cold War and the need for safe information storage and communications (Hobbes, 2002; Randall,

1997; Segaller, 1999). However, when it comes to tracing the development of ideas behind the Internet and the WWW, Vannevar Bush (1945) is usually credited for planting the conceptual seed (Cailliau, 1995; S. Johnson, 1997; Packer & Jordan, 2001; Stewart, 2002).

Bush's (1945) inspiring idea consisted of a machine for indexing, storing, and retrieving information. This machine, called the memex, was intended to be a personal storage and filing system in the shape of a desk. The desk would be fitted with projection screens, a keyboard and various levers for controlling the display of information, which would be stored on microfiche-type film. The revolutionary idea in this entire system was that the memex would make it possible to establish associative links between microfiche documents and to index information associatively, mimicking the way people think, which is by association. The links or trails of information created by memex users could be stored for later reference. The idea of associative trails of information anticipated the hyperlink and had great influence on later developments.

Another influential thinker in the development of the World Wide Web is the creator of the terms *hyperlink* and *hypertext*, Ted Nelson (Packer & Jordan, 2001; Stewart, 2002). Nelson, who was trained in philosophy and sociology, first coined the term *hypertext* in the 1960s to refer to nonsequential, nonlinear writing (Nelson, 1987). In Nelson's conceptualization, hypertext was not necessarily computer-bound, but computers facilitated writing in interrelated (linked) chunks of text. Nelson had the vision of a *grand hypertext* which would encompass all the hypertexts ever written on a subject. To this day, he is still trying to realize his dream with Project Xanadu (http://xanadu.com). Project Xanadu, if ever accomplished, would be another type of World Wide Web, designed according to Nelson's philosophy about nonsequential writing and fair access to information. Hypertext and hyperlinks, however, have proven to be very influential concepts and are today the basis of the World Wide Web.

No history of the World Wide Web would be complete without an overview of the technological developments that lead to the computer network that makes the WWW possible. The history of the initial computer network that later became the Internet is complex, with many contributions being made by several people, and ideas being developed simultaneously in different places. It is widely-known that the first computer network, ARPAnet, was developed by the Advanced Research Projects Agency (ARPA), an agency of the U.S. Department of Defense. ARPA was an initiative taken during the Cold War in response to the U.S.S.R.'s launching of the Sputnik satellite (Segaller, 1999). Although ARPA was supposed to do cutting-edge research that would give the United States an advantage in the Cold War, the motivation behind the creation of ARPAnet is not clearly military. Some sources claim that ARPA was trying to find a solution for reliable information storage and communications that would resist a nuclear attack (Stewart, 2002). Others claim that ARPAnet was developed to save money by enabling resource and information sharing among a limited number of very expensive computers, and that scientists working on the network did not have military purposes in mind (Segaller, 1999; Wood & Smith, 2001). Only Paul Baran justified his work on packet switching in a distributed network as a potential defense against nuclear attacks, but at the time Baran was not associated with ARPA (Segaller, 1999). The intentions behind the development of the Internet are important because they shaped the Internet and influenced what it has become, and they can help us understand the spirit, soul, (Randall, 1997) or technical code (Flanagin, Farinola, & Metzger, 2002) of the

Internet. Although it is not clear whether the motivation behind the creation of ARPAnet (later the Internet) was military or civilian, one point that its creators seem to agree on is that they wanted to devise a *communication* network (Randall, 1997). Besides intentions, the technical foundations of the Internet greatly influenced the network's later development. Two of these foundational ideas are Baran's notion of distributed networks and Cerf's Transport Control Protocol (TCP)/Internet Protocol (IP).

Baran's work, developed independently of ARPA, but later coopted and used in the creation of ARPAnet, proposed a network topography that would ensure proper functioning and communication among computers even in the case that one or more machines would be destroyed. In 1964 he proposed a distributed network structure, in which there would be no major centers, and all the vital functions would be distributed among outposts (Segaller, 1999). This network structure was used in the creation of ARPAnet and is the structure of today's Internet. This type of structure makes it impossible to stop or control the network from any particular point, because the network is not dependent on any one node for proper functioning. If a node is not functional, data packets will not get stuck; they will switch routes and get to their destination anyway (hence, "packet switching"). The distributed network structure of the Internet is not just a set of technical specifications of no interest to communication scholars. The structure of the Internet is interesting because it may help explain the nature of Internet communication, and even recent debates over the difficulty (or even impossibility) of controlling and regulating the Internet. The technical structure of the Internet might account for the decentralized and somewhat anarchic nature of Internet communication.

The second major technical idea that actually transformed ARPAnet into the Internet we know today is Cerf's TCP/IP (Segaller, 1999). After ARPAnet was created in 1969, and more and more computers from major universities and corporations joined the network, communication among computers became difficult because they were using different languages and operating systems. TCP/IP is, in very simple terms, a common language and a buffer zone, that different machines can be programmed to understand so that they can speak to each other. The switch to TCP/IP was officially made on January 1, 1983, which is considered the birthday of the Internet (Randall, 1997). TCP/IP made it possible for ARPAnet to grow and to interconnect with several other computer networks around the globe. These *internet*worked networks formed the Internet. The ideology underlying TCP/IP can be interpreted as one of open communication, a common language that grants access to everyone and allows large numbers of people to join in. TCP/IP ensures that resource and information sharing will function properly regardless of the types and numbers of participating computers.

The early Internet was very different from the Internet we see today. The interfaces were text-based, and one had to type commands in order to perform actions on remote computers. The World Wide Web changed the Internet into a predominantly graphic interface. The notion of graphic interface itself was a major development at the time and is another foundational idea in the development of the WWW as we know it today.

The graphic user interface (GUI) was the creation of Doug Engelbart, a navy officer who was inspired by Bush's idea of the memex. Engelbart believed that computing technology can be used to augment human intellect and he set out to develop such technologies. The major breakthrough came in 1968, when, at a computer conference, he presented a "tool kit" that included windows for editing text, graphic manipulation of information, and a small device called a mouse (Packer & Jordan, 2001). Engelbart's essential contribution has enabled computer users to visualize and manipulate information by virtually reaching through the interface. For example, instead of typing a command asking the computer to move a fragment of text to another location, one can virtually reach through the interface and drag the text across the computer screen to its new location. Engelbart's invention is at the basis of point-and-click, "what you see is what you get" (WYSIWYG) software applications, and of the World Wide Web.

The World Wide Web itself was initially a browser, a software application developed by Tim Berners-Lee at CERN (European Laboratory for Particle Physics) to facilitate the storage and linking of research papers. The software was initially developed for CERN, although Berners-Lee anticipated it could be used to solve information management problems "in the rest of the world" (Berners-Lee, as cited in Randall, 1997, p. 184). Berners-Lee envisioned a system that would be available on the Internet to the entire world, would work on different platforms, and support various data formats. He worked on the project through 1991, when the first Web server was launched at CERN; and he insisted that the code for the World Wide Web be open source, so it could be further developed and improved by individuals throughout the world. In 1994 the World Wide Web Consortium (W3C) was created, to develop technology and standards for the Web and ensure its accessibility. Berners-Lee still heads the W3C today.

Berners-Lee was a visionary who coined terms that have become part of everyday language, such as *browser* and *navigation* (referring to the Web). Berners-Lee envisioned and fought for some values that have become embedded in Web technology: wide and open access, cross-platform compatibility, support of multiple data formats (which makes multimedia on the Web possible), flexibility, and adaptability.

Many other people made important contributions to the development of the World Wide Web and this short account does not do them justice. The purpose of this section was not to write an exhaustive history of the WWW (excellent detailed accounts are available elsewhere), but to point out the key ideas that shaped the nature, or the spirit of the World Wide Web and that in turn influence communication via this medium. This short history shows that the values of inter-connectedness, open access, ease of use, and communication were at the basis of the creation of the Web and are likely to have influenced the way we communicate on the WWW today. But before discussing WWW communication, it is necessary to gain a basic understanding of what the Web is, and how it works.

Understanding WWW Technologies
The World Wide Web is made up of computer files sitting on computers with a permanent Internet connection. These computers are called Web servers. Web users employ special computer programs—called browsers—such as Mozilla Firefox or Internet Explorer, to access Web pages. Browsers communicate with servers and request that specific files be transferred to the browser and displayed on the user's computer. The communication protocol used by browsers and servers is called hypertext transfer protocol (HTTP). A specific page from a server is requested by typing the file's location, or uniform resource locator (URL) into the browser. URLs are addresses that uniquely identify each page on the WWW and its location. For example, typing in the URL icdweb.cc.purdue.edu/~mihaela/index.html

will request that the file index.html, located on a Purdue (purdue) University (edu) Computing Center (cc) server called icdweb, in the user account "mihaela," be transferred to the browser and displayed on the computer. More detailed and technical accounts of how the WWW works can be found in sources such as Randall (1997), Stewart (2002), Wilde (1999), and Wood and Smith (2001).

Although Web pages are usually files of certain types (html, asp, etc.), the Web is not limited to certain data formats. The original language for scripting Web pages—hypertext markup language (HTML)—as well as more recent Web page scripting languages, can incorporate other file formats such as images, sound, animation, data bases, and so forth. These technologies make it possible for Web sites to be rich, dynamic, and interactive multimedia environments.

A Web site is a collection of interlinked and interrelated pages that are usually hosted on the same server and authored by the same entity. Individual Web pages need to be linked to form a Web site. A link contains the URL of the page to be downloaded when the user clicks it. In links, the URL is usually masked by text or pictures, but in essence it is the same URL one would type in the browser's address bar to download that page.

Web pages are authored by either writing computer script or using special WYSIWYG editors. Examples of popular Web page editors are Macromedia Dreamweaver, Microsoft Frontpage, and Netscape Composer. Recent technology allows Web pages to feed from databases and update their contents automatically depending on variables such as time, user preferences, and so forth. Initially a relatively simple technology, Web sites are increasingly complex. The task of creating a Web site has become less like text editing and more like computer programming. However, Web pages are very flexible media because the technology allows virtually unlimited combinations and variations of individual elements. This flexibility allows Web authors to make many choices when creating a site. These choices, some argue, are rhetorical. The next section reviews ideas about the rhetoric of electronic text, hypertext, and hypermedia that will help identify and better understand the unique characteristics of WWW communication.

WWW Communication

Rhetorical approaches to electronic media provide useful insight into the nature of Web-based communication. A lot has been written about various electronic media and hypertext, and although Web communication does not fall neatly into either of these two categories, it shares some important characteristics with each of them. Because the Web is in part electronic text, hypertext, multimedia, and graphic interface, we can transfer some knowledge about these media to it. This section reviews rhetorical and stylistic approaches to electronic media that inform Web-based communication. The author, the text, and the reader of electronic texts and hypertexts are three main foci in this body of literature.

The Author

Electronic hypertext, defined as computer-based nonlinear writing, is viewed as a very flexible and deeply rhetorical medium that offers authors ample opportunities for expression (Lanham, 1992, 1993; Soukup, 2000). In the past, printing technologies made it difficult for authors to engage visual aspects of texts such as layout and typography. Now, because electronic texts are flexible and easy to change, they bring visual elements back into the author's repertoire of expression (Landow, 1997; Lanham, 1992, 1993). Besides the rhetorical possibilities offered by editorial aspects of the text, the capability of electronic texts to support multimedia (visual, audio, and video messages) also enhances authorial expression (Lanham, 1992, 1993; Packer & Jordan, 2001). Other characteristics of electronic text that deeply influence the nature of communication in this medium are discussed next.

The Text

Web sites are complex, rich multimedia texts characterized by nonlinearity, interactivity, openness, and decentralization. These characteristics set Web sites apart from most print texts. Lanham (1992) considered electronic text a new rhetorical environment because it is a complex medium that offers multiple possibilities for expression. Electronic text, created and read with the help of a computer, is deeply rhetorical because it can be very easily modified. The computer makes editorial and production changes so easy that they become rhetorical (Lanham, 1992). Lanham argued that by modifying the appearance of text, its meaning is also altered.

Similarly, Web sites are complex, flexible media that offer enormous possibilities for variation. As opposed to a book or a pamphlet, where the variations are limited and difficult to implement once the text has been printed, Web sites offer great possibilities for variation and combination of elements, both before and after publication. Web site elements (or their combination) can be altered at any point, which provides an almost infinite array of rhetorical choices. For example, imagine keeping the content (verbal arguments and photographs) identical and varying the layout, the chromatic scheme, the navigation solution, and the overall structure of a site. The result will be a new communication artifact that offers a different experience and contributes to the creation of different meanings. Electronic text is a fluid, living text because it is never finished and it can be changed even after publication (Landow, 1997; Lanham, 1992, 1993).

The electronic text environment, according to Lanham, brings together the communicative power of verbal communication, structure, and interactivity. Other authors (e.g., Soukup, 2000) also argued that electronic multimedia is a complete and unique communication context, rich and fully dynamic, that requires new theories and methods of analysis. The term "rhetorical environment" is an appropriate alternative to the word *text* in the discussion of Web sites. This is why in this project I do not refer to Web sites as texts, but as communication environments in which Web site users live rhetorical experiences. The Web site communication environment is also nonlinear, open, and decentralized.

The most often mentioned characteristic of hypertext, which Web sites borrow, is nonlinearity. Authors write that hypertext is nonlinear, nonsequential, fragmented, and dispersed (Aarseth, 1997; Bush, 1945; Landow, 1997; Nelson, 1987, 1992; Packer & Jordan, 2001; Slatin, 1991). Hypertext is composed of discrete blocks of text. The blocks of text are interconnected by links created by the author; and, in the case of genuine hypertext, also by readers (Bush, 1945; Landow, 1997; Nelson, 1992).

The constitutive blocks of hypertext can be accessed in any order, which makes it interactive, open, and decentralized. Hypertext is open, because it does not have a predetermined beginning and end. Multiple beginnings and ends are possible, depending upon the reader's chosen path (Landow, 1997; Slatin, 1991). Hypertext is decentralized, or has an ever-migrating centrality. Because hypertext is experienced in nonlinear and unpredictable ways, it is never clear what parts are central and which are secondary. The status of parts potentially changes from central to secondary with every reading (Landow, 1997). The complexity, richness, nonlinearity, interactivity, and openness of Web sites create a communication environment that provides readers/ visitors with novel rhetorical experiences and in the process change the very nature of the act of reading. These changes are discussed next.

The Reader

The reader of hypertext differs in important ways from the reader of print media or the audience of mass media such as radio and television. While all these other media imply a relatively passive receiver, the hypertext reader is active, or even intrusive (Landow, 1997; Nelson, 1987; Slatin, 1991). Hypertext requires the active participation of the reader who, at the very least, chooses paths through information; and in some hypertext systems such as Storyspace and Intermedia, is able to add links and make annotations. Web 2.0 applications that allow bookmarking, tagging, and sharing also allow active participation and blend the acts of reading and content creation. Aarseth (1997) used the metaphor of the *voyeur* to refer to the reader of print texts and feels that the *player* metaphor better reflects the act of reading hypertext. Hypertext also empowers readers because it provides easy access to a wealth of interconnected information, thus contributing to democratization and the dissemination of knowledge and power (Bush, 1945; Landow, 1997; Nelson, 1987, 1992).

The interactive experience of hypertext can be engaging, playful, and immersive (Lanham, 1992, 1993; Packer & Jordan, 2001). Sometimes, the distinction between play and purpose is blurred because accomplishing goals through engaged participation is enjoyable (Lanham, 1992, 1993; Laurel, 1991; Nielsen, 2002). Hypertexts, especially multimedia ones, stimulate a feeling of immersion in a three-dimensional environment and create a sense of space (McPhee, 1997; Packer & Jordan, 2001). The drawback of feeling immersed in a (virtual) space is a sense of disorientation and being lost (Aarseth, 1997; Brinck et al., 2002; Landow, 1997; Nielsen, 2000a).

Reading electronic texts is an active, playful, immersive, empowering, disorienting, and therefore, different rhetorical experience. The characteristics of the hypertext reading experience have rhetorical functions. For example, in his hypertext novel, *Afternoon, A Story*, author Michael Joyce makes purposeful, rhetorical use of interactivity, open-endedness, and disorientation (Joyce, 1990).

In short, Web-based communication shares with electronic text and hypertext a number of characteristics: It is nonlinear, interactive, playful, and fluid. It is deeply rhetorical because it offers more possibilities for expression and interpretation than print. It empowers readers by enabling easy access to massive quantities of information and it provides an immersive, engaging, but sometimes disorienting rhetorical experience. The next section explores what we already know about people's experiences using Web sites.

Online User Experiences and Behaviors
Online user behavior and Web site usability studies provide some insight into what goes on as users experience Web sites. Research shows that Web site use in general is a rapidly interactive activity. A study based on user log data analysis concluded that people are hurried Web users, and spend an average of only a few seconds on each Web page (Cockburn & McKenzie, 2001). Findings from Web site usability research seem to support this conclusion. Based on his studies and observations, usability expert Jakob Nielsen concluded that it takes users less than 10

seconds to form an impression of a page (Nielsen, 2000d, 2001c; Nielsen & Norman, 2000). Studies show that on the Web, people do not read, they quickly scan pages (Morkes & Nielsen, 1997). Overall, users are impatient with slow sites that take a long time to download and respond (Nielsen, 1999a, 2000a; Nielsen & Norman, 2000).

The main drawback of the experience provided by hypertext, as discussed earlier, is disorientation. User behavior and Web usability research support this conclusion. Eveland and Dunwoody (2000) conducted a study in an academic setting confirming that maintaining orientation while browsing the Web is the cognitive task that takes up more than half of users' mental resources. In the study, 62% of think-aloud comments indicated that people engaged in orientation maintenance, 25% indicated the cognitive task of elaboration, and only 13% referred to evaluation of content.

Much, if not most, of this research focuses on behaviors related to navigation and maintaining orientation. After all, clear and efficient navigation is fundamental to accomplishing the main purpose that makes people turn to the Web—to find information. Some studies that explore the general patterns users engage in to find information are discussed next.

A report of the National Cancer Institute, sponsor of the respected Web site usability.gov, summarizes research on how people search information on the Web (Koyani & Bailey, 2002). The report compares two methods of finding information: targeted searching—using a search engine provided by a Web site—and following links. The data reviewed show that more than 50% of users prefer searching, 20% prefer linking, and 30% exhibit mixed behaviors. However, linking is overall more effective in helping people find the information they need. Individual preferences and type of Web site were not good predictors of which information-finding behavior users engaged in. Instead, users who knew well what they were looking for picked searching, whereas those who knew only the broad category of information (i.e., digital cameras) chose linking.

Brinck et al. (2002) also believed that the type of task users try to accomplish determines the navigation style they engage in: searching, linking, sampling various pages, or making sure they read each page. The authors review a number of frequently discussed navigation models: omniscience, optimal rationality, satisficing, mental maps, route memorization, information foraging, and information costs. The models represent different navigation behaviors and vary in their assumptions about human knowledge, motivation to review alternatives, and risk taking. The omniscience model is the one of the ideal user who has a perfect mental representation of the Web site and is able to take the most efficient path to information. The optimal rationality model assumes that people have limited knowledge, but that they are always able to pick the most effective alternative. The satisficing model represents users who make decisions based only on immediately available information and avoid remembering information or planning ahead. The mental map model is based on evidence that users form a mental model of the Web site and take the path that makes sense according to their mental model. Route memorization involves repeated use of a navigation path that has worked in the past. The information foraging model portrays users who try to get as much information as possible at one location before choosing an alternative. Finally, the information costs model assumes that users make tradeoffs to decide what mental resources to apply and therefore what information finding strategy to utilize.

Usability research shows that overall, navigation is a difficult task and that about one-third of the time even experienced users cannot find the information they are looking for (Nielsen, 2003a, 2003b). Even if findings about navigation patterns do not always provide definitive answers, they do provide quite a lot of insight into how people look for information on Web sites. This is not the case with other aspects of the Web user experience, which we know almost nothing about. A more rounded account of the Web user experience is required, one that will address not only navigation, but also other aspects of this experience. Research is needed to explore various facets of the Web user experience and to connect users' behaviors and perceptions with Web design. To be able to make this connection, it is important to understand the main elements of Web site design. These are reviewed next.

WEB SITE DESIGN

Guidelines for effective and easy-to-use Web site design abound. Amazon.com offers over 8,000 titles about Web site design. Although it is virtually impossible and hardly necessary to compile a comprehensive review of the Web design literature, a few major ideas are discussed here. The purpose of this section is not to provide an extensive list of guidelines for effective Web site design, but to use Web design literature to identify the most important constitutive elements of Web sites.

Without exception, all the Web style guides reviewed here (Brinck et al., 2002; IBM, 2003b; Lynch & Horton, 2002; Nielsen, 2000a; Nielsen & Loranger, 2006; Van Duyne, Landay, & Hong, 2003) share the perspective of user-centered design. The main principle behind their recommendations is usability, defined as ease-of-use of the Web site. They all emphasize the requirements of simplicity, clarity, predictability, speed, and consistency in the design of Web sites.

Another aspect the Web design books have in common is the range of topics they cover. Each book dedicates chapters to page design and layout, site structure, organization and navigation, writing for the Web, and using multimedia and graphics. Some style manuals also address the Web site planning and development process (IBM, 2003b; Lynch & Horton, 2002), usability evaluation (Brinck et al., 2002; IBM, 2003b), intranet design (Nielsen, 2000a), and sometimes special topics such as issues specific to e-commerce sites (IBM, 2003b; Van Duyne et al., 2003).

Besides guidelines for easy-to-use Web designs, Van Duyne et al. (2003) presented two novel ideas. The first is a list of Web site genres, comprising eleven categories: e-commerce, news, community conference, self-service government, nonprofits, grassroots information sites, company sites, educational forums, arts and entertainment, Web applications, and intranets. Although their list is not comprehensive (for example, national self-presentation Web sites do not fit in any of the eleven genres), the idea of identifying Web site genres might prove very fruitful.

The second intriguing idea Van Duyne et al. (2003) discussed is that of patterns. They broke down the content of their book in small units and label each unit a pattern, arguing that Web designers can choose patterns and combine them as needed. Although the nature of the patterns in the book is inconsistent (some examples of patterns are: Web site genres, navigation styles, site branding, page templates, and action buttons), the idea that Web sites can be built out of different combinations of given elements is a useful one. The question emerges: What are the most basic elements that Web sites can be made of? The topics addressed in these Web design manuals can be used to compile a list of constitutive elements of Web sites: content (verbal, visual, and multimedia), graphic design (layout and typography), and navigation (links and organizational elements) seem to be the basic building blocks of Web sites. This understanding of Web site components will be useful in the construction of a framework that combines the subjective Web user experience and the design aspect of sites. Before beginning the discussion of a new theoretical framework of the Web user experience, the next section examines how this experience has been approached in previous communication-oriented empirical research.

RESEARCHING THE WWW: COMMUNICATION STUDIES

This section reviews a number of communication-based empirical studies of Web sites with the purpose of learning about the methodologies and theoretical perspectives employed. Most of the studies considered for the purpose of this review are exploratory in nature and employ content analysis to identify the core characteristics of various kinds of Web sites or textual analysis to gain a deeper understanding of the rhetorical strategies used mostly for self-presentation. Few studies are theory driven, and some studies employ methodologies driven by improvised frameworks. These three groups of studies are discussed next.

Exploratory Content Analytic Studies

Many exploratory content analyses focus on corporate Web sites in order to assess what kinds of topics and audiences corporations address on the Web (Aikat, 2000; Chaudhri & Wang, 2007; Esrock & Leichty, 1998, 1999, 2000; Maynard & Tian, 2004; Tian, 2006), or how they practice media relations online (Alfonso & de Valbuena Miguel, 2006; Callison, 2003; Esrock & Leichty, 1999). Another category of sites about which general exploratory questions are answered with the help of content analysis are political candidates' and representatives' Web sites. Researchers have studied topics such as the kind of images politicians put forth (Lipinski & Neddenriep, 2004; Niven & Zilber, 2001), use of negative advertising in electoral campaigns (Klotz, 1998), and the effectiveness of channel use (Reavy, 1997). Exploratory content analysis has also been used to study international public relations (Curtin & Gaither, 2003; Mohammed, 2004), university Web sites (Kuchi, 2006; E. M. Will & Callison, 2006), environmental, crisis, and risk management Web sites (Capriotti, 2007; Fisher Liu, 2008; Perry, Taylor, & Doerfel, 2003; Pinterits, Treiblmaier, & Pollach, 2006), nonprofit organizations' Web sites (Kang & Norton, 2004) and personal home pages (Dominick, 1999; Papacharissi, 2002). As a body of research, these exploratory content analyses identify content categories and sometimes message strategies and other features of Web sites. The purpose of most exploratory content analyses is to identify and count the types of content, or types of messages, published on Web sites. This body of research contributes important information about how Web sites are used by different organizations, companies, nation-states, and individuals. However, due to their exploratory nature, these studies contribute very little in terms of theory development. In fact, a meta-analysis of 674 communication journal articles about the Internet revealed that most communication Internet research is atheoretical (S. T. Kim & Weaver, 2002).

Not all studies of Web sites are purely exploratory and atheoretical. Some studies, such as those discussed in the following section, attempt to answer research questions derived from theoretical perspectives.

Theory-Driven Studies
A body of research is evolving around Kent & Taylor's (1998) five dialogic principles of Web site design. The studies in this

body of research follow the same methodological approach: They use content analysis to evaluate Web site content and design features and attempt to contact the Web site authors to assess responsiveness. This evaluation of Web sites' use of the five dialogic principles has been performed on activist Web sites (Kent et al., 2003; Taylor et al., 2001), and congressional Web sites (Taylor & Kent, 2004), to name a few. The five dialogic principles are proposed by the authors based on public relations and dialogic theory, but they are not a theory, just a set of principles that can be applied to evaluate Web sites.

Public relations theories, such as excellence theory (J. E. Grunig & Hunt, 1984; J. E. Grunig & IABC Research Foundation., 1992; L. A. Grunig, Grunig, & Dozier, 2002) and relationship management theory (Ledingham, 2003), have been used to guide content analyses of corporate (Jo & Jung, 2005; Ki & Hon, 2006), activist (Reber & Kim, 2006), and litigation public relations (Reber & Kim, 2006) Web sites.

Other examples of theory-driven studies of Web sites are Jackson and Purcell's (1997) analysis of representations of former Yugoslavia, which employed media richness theory; M. Will and Porak's (2000) analysis of corporate communication on the Web, which utilized a previously proposed corporate communication model; McMillan's (1999) study of health Web sites based on a conceptual definition of interactivity, as well as a number of textual analyses of Web sites grounded in rhetorical theory (Fursich & Robins, 2002, 2004; Zhang & Benoit, 2004).

The theory-driven studies reviewed here contribute new knowledge about the application of public relations and other theories to Web sites. However, they share two important limitations: They only apply, but do not build theory about Web site communication; and they approach Web sites as texts, ignoring Web site users and their experience using Web sites. Very few studies go beyond content or textual analysis, such as Naude, Froneman, and Atwood's (2004) study, which used interviews with the public relations practitioners responsible for South African nongovernmental agencies' Web sites to complement their analyses of the Web sites. Another study used a survey to ask Taiwanese journalists about their perceptions and use of political candidates' Web sites (Chen, 2007).

Although Web sites are fruitful topics of communication research, most studies are either exploratory or atheoretical; they apply, but do not build theory, and approach Web sites as texts, not as experiences. Very few researchers have attempted to build frameworks, methods, or theory about Web site communication. These attempts are reviewed next.

Frameworks and Methods for Web Site Analysis

The most notable body of research on Web sites that uses rigorous methodology is the one conducted at the Stanford Web Credibility Lab. For the past few years, the Stanford Web Credibility Lab has focused on what aspects of Web sites increase their perceived credibility. The research uses survey and experimental Web-based methods. The survey methods consist of lists of statements about various Web site aspects, which respondents rate for the likelihood to make a Web site more or less credible. An example of such a statement is "The Web site provides a contact phone number." All statements are rated on a much less believable—much more believable scale (Fogg, Kameda et al., 2002). The experimental method developed at Stanford presents participants with two Web sites and asks them to evaluate their credibility. Participants are asked to provide overall credibility ratings and open-ended evaluations of the sites (Fogg, Marable, Stanford, & Tauber, 2002; Fogg, Marshall, Kameda, Solomon, & Rangnekar, 2002). The Web site credibility body of research is driven by the utilitarian purposes of learning how to judge Web site credibility and how to make Web sites more credible. However, one theory about site credibility has also resulted from this approach. Prominence-interpretation theory (PIT) explains that credibility assessments are a function of the interaction of a site element's prominence (whether it is noticed) and the value judgment users make about it (Fogg, 2003).

The Cyberspace Policy Research Group has developed a coding scheme to be used for evaluating the transparency and interactivity of public agency or government Web sites (Cyberspace Policy Research Group, 2001). It is not clear how the coding scheme was developed, although the authors state it was based on collected data. Also not clear is why transparency and interactivity are the only two aspects of Web sites worth investigating. The Cyberspace Policy Research Group is concerned with online democracy, and the openness of government bureaucracies' Web sites. It is possible that transparency and interactivity are the Web site aspects most relevant to openness. The coding scheme, known as the Web site attribute evaluation system, is a very comprehensive rating sheet that has been used to evaluate several agencies' Web sites. However, the rating sheets evaluate Web sites as texts, and not the user experience. Also, although the rating sheet is research based, it has not resulted in any theory or theoretical framework.

Bennett (2005) studied Web site atmospherics—the emotional response charity Web sites can elicit in users and its consequences. Bennett proposed an elaborate model of Web site atmospherics which was only partially supported by data. However, the study showed that a charity Web site's openness, novelty, and complexity influence the user experience, the Web site users' mood, and approach or avoidance behavior. Bennett's research proposed a theoretical model and focused on users' experiences and perceptions, and as such presents an ideal example of the direction future communication research should take.

Benoit and Benoit (2000) described and evaluated the Web sites of the main political candidates for the 2000 Presidential Election. The authors provided a comprehensive rating sheet with categories specific to political candidates' Web sites and used this rating sheet to assign scores to Web sites. The authors did not explain how they created the scale, why the categories were chosen, or how their relative weight was decided.

Huizingh (2000) developed a research framework, later updated by Robbins and Stylianou (2003), used to analyze and categorize the capabilities of commercial Web sites. The framework distinguishes between structure and content of a Web site and between objective features and user perceptions at both the structure and the content levels. It is a combination of content analysis and subjective ratings on several dimensions listed by the authors under the categories of content and design, respectively. Similar to Benoit and Benoit's (2000) rating sheet, the framework records the presence or absence of various content and design elements, such as information about specific products, information about the company, search engines, and so forth.

DiNardo (2002) used an Internet information management model to rate the quality of four Web site elements: content, ease of use and navigation, interactive communication, and timeliness of information. No rationale is provided by DiNardo about the inclusion of these aspects in the evaluation of Web sites.

With the possible exception of the Stanford Web credibility research, these approaches to Web site research present serious problems. From a communication perspective, the presence, absence, and even quality of certain content categories or design elements is not very informative in the absence of meanings Web site users create from this absence or presence. By saying that Web site A is a 5 and Web site B is a 7, we miss out on the rhetorical choices made in these Web sites as they are experienced by users. Such frameworks are useful for assessing the types of content, design elements, and technological features present on Web sites and for evaluating the choices made by the Web site authors. They lack depth, however, and do not address the user experience of visiting Web sites. Moreover, the tools reviewed here are not really models or frameworks of Web sites. According to Hawes (1975), a model is a representation of a phenomenon, and a theoretical framework includes a series of concepts and the relationships among them. None of the tools discussed here represent Web sites or the Web user experience, nor do they define a set of concepts and their relationships—therefore, they are little more than rating sheets. The communication discipline needs a more disciplined (pun intended) approach to the experience of visiting Web sites. A framework of the public relations Web site experience can contribute to meeting this need. As established earlier, the experience of visiting public relations Web sites is characterized by relationship building and maintenance. The following section reviews conceptual and theoretical public relations insights about building and maintaining relationships between organizations and publics.

ORGANIZATION-PUBLIC RELATIONSHIPS

Many public relations scholars, regardless of the particular approach they take to the study of the discipline, agree that the purpose of public relations is to build and maintain positive relationships between organizations and their publics (Botan, 1992; Broom et al., 1997, 2000; Center & Jackson, 1995; J. E. Grunig & Huang, 2000; Hallahan, 2003; Heath, 2000; Kent & Taylor, 1998; Ledingham, 2003, 2006; Ledingham & Bruning, 1998). Some scholars focus on the relationship aspect of public relations and have developed what is known as "the relationship approach" as a general theory of public relations (Broom et al., 2000; J. E. Grunig & Huang, 2000; Ledingham, 2003, 2006; Ledingham & Bruning, 1998). The relationship approach to public relations provides useful insights about the nature of organization-public relationships, ways to build and maintain these relationships, and the role the WWW can play in organization-public relationships.

The Nature of Organization-Public Relationships

Although relatively new, the relationship approach to public relations has benefited from scholarly attention and research that have successfully laid its foundations. Various conceptualizations and models of organization-public relationships have been advanced, methods for assessing relationships have been created, and the research has also produced different ways of classifying relationships.

Concepts and Models

The beginnings of the systematic study of organization-public relationships can be traced to Broom et al.'s (1997) conceptual framework of antecedents and consequences of relationships (Ledingham, 2003). Broom et al. attempted to explain the concept of organization-public relationship and provided a framework for understanding how relationships are formed and how they affect organizations. The model of relationships antecedents and consequences has been adopted by other public relations scholars (e.g., J. E. Grunig & Huang, 2000). According to this view, relationships are influenced by preexisting conditions such as perceptions, expectations, norms, necessity, and so forth. In turn, positive long-term relationships between organizations and publics have a number of beneficial consequences, such as goal achievement, control mutuality, commitment, satisfaction, and so forth (Broom et al., 1997; Bruning, 2002; Bruning & Ledingham, 1998; J. E. Grunig & Huang, 2000). Whereas there is little debate about the antecedents-consequences model of organization-public relationships, the notion of relationship itself and the dimensions that define a good relationship gave rise to more diverse conceptualizations.

Broom et al. (1997) proposed a dynamic view of relationships as exchanges, or transfers of information, energy, or resources. Therefore, they claimed, the quality of the organization-public relationship is indicated by the characteristics of the exchanges, transactions, communications, and other interconnected activities of organizations and publics.

Ledingham and Bruning (1998) set out to identify key dimensions or organization-public relationships. They identified several dimensions of relationships in different bodies of literature and found out that only five of them—trust, commitment, involvement, investment, and openness—distinguish between customers who decide to keep the services of a company and those who do not. These five dimensions of relationships have been confirmed and used in other studies by the same authors (Bruning & Ledingham, 1998, 2000; Ledingham, 2003; Ledingham & Bruning, 1999, 2000).

Ledingham and Bruning proposed a view of relationships somewhat different from Broom et al.'s (1997). They did not conceptualize relationships as exchanges and transactions; instead, they defined an organization-public relationship as: "The state which exists between an organization and its key publics in which the actions of either entity impact the economic, social, political and/or cultural well-being of the other entity" (Ledingham & Bruning, 1998, p. 62). J. E. Grunig and Huang (2000) saw this state of interdependence as an antecedent to organization-public relationships. They believed that because organizations' and publics' behaviors influence each other, they are motivated to build relationships. J. E. Grunig and Huang brought excellence theory to improve Broom et al.'s (1997) model of antecedents and consequences to relationships. Instead of defining the relationship concept, J. E. Grunig and Huang listed symmetrical and asymmetrical relationship maintenance and conflict resolution strategies, which might indicate that they also viewed relationships as transactions, both symbolic and behavioral (J. E. Grunig, 1993), not as states. Examples of symmetrical relationship maintenance strategies are disclosure, assurances of legitimacy, participation in common networks, sharing tasks, and so forth. The consequences of relationship building, according to J. E. Grunig and Huang, are good relationships defined by characteristics such as control mutuality, trust, relational satisfaction, and relational commitment (J. E. Grunig, 2002; J. E. Grunig & Huang, 2000; Hon & J. E. Grunig, 1999).

Assessment of Organization-Public Relationships
Besides creating conceptual models of organization-public relationships, public relations scholars have also been concerned with finding ways to measure relationships. Relationships can be measured either by assessing the participants' perceptions (co-orientational measures), or by looking at factors independent of the participants, such as characteristics of their transactions. Broom et al. (1997) advocated the latter approach, stating that relationships can be evaluated by looking at characteristics of the participants' communication linkage: symmetry, intensity, content, frequency, valence, and duration. Ledingham and Bruning (Bruning, 2002; Bruning & Ledingham, 1998, 1999, 2000; Ledingham & Bruning, 1998, 2000) looked at the public's and organization members' perceptions when measuring relationships.

J. E. Grunig and his colleagues advocated a mixed approach, although they have focused on developing a relationship measurement scale that looks at participants' perceptions of relationship dimensions (J. E. Grunig, 2002; Hon & J. E. Grunig, 1999). As a result of this research, several instruments for measuring organization-public relationships exist in the literature. The scale developed by Bruning and Ledingham measures the relationship dimensions of trust, commitment, involvement, investment, and openness (Bruning, 2002; Bruning & Ledingham, 1998, 1999, 2000; Ledingham & Bruning, 1998, 2000). Another scale, developed by J. E. Grunig and his colleagues, assesses the relationship outcomes of trust, control mutuality, commitment, and satisfaction (J. E. Grunig, 2002; J. E. Grunig & Huang, 2000; Hon & J. E. Grunig, 1999). Huang (2001) adapted this scale to an international environment, and added the dimension of face and favor to J. E. Grunig and colleagues' four dimensions, thus proposing a five-dimension scale, OPRA. Kim (2001) started afresh and analyzed over 100 relationship-related items in order to build an organization-public relationship scale. Exploratory and confirmatory factor analyses resulted in a 16-item scale, assessing four relationship dimensions: trust, commitment, local or community involvement, and reputation.

Because this research project is different in many ways from the research contexts for which these relationship assessment scales were created, simply adopting one of them for use here would be inappropriate for at least two reasons. First, this study does not aim to measure the relationship between an organization and a public, rather it inquires about how relationships are built online. Second, because this project aims to create a descriptive framework of the public relations Web site experience, it needs to employ open-ended questions that will produce qualitative data about the Web site experience rather than about the sponsoring organization. So, the relationship scales described in the literature cannot be simply adopted, but they can and do inform this project by providing relevant dimensions of organization-public relationships. For the purpose of this research, it will be necessary to select the most relevant dimensions and to formulate appropriate questions to assess each dimension in the online context.

Typologies of Organization-Public Relationships
The research of organization-public relationships has also produced two typologies of relationships. One typology is the result of a factor analysis of items used to measure relationship dimensions and distinguishes among personal, professional, and community relationships (Bruning & Ledingham, 1999). Personal relationships describe the organization dealing with public members as individuals. Professional relationships involve meeting customer needs efficiently; community relationships focus on the organization's commitment to its neighboring community. An organization can have more than one type of relationship with one public at the same moment in time, which points to the multidimensionality of organization-public relationships.

Another typology of organization-public relationships distinguishes between exchange and communal relationships (J. E. Grunig, 2002; Hon & J. E. Grunig, 1999). Exchange relationships are based on reciprocity, "one party gives benefits to the other only because the other has provided benefits in the past or is expected to do so in the future" (J. E. Grunig, 2002, p. 1). Communal relationships are characterized by a concern with the general welfare of the other party, regardless of the absence of (immediate) benefits.

Existing research shows that relationships are complex and multidimensional concepts, which can be understood and measured in different ways. Regardless of how relationships are conceptualized, researchers agree that positive relationships are beneficial to both the public and the organization. But how are long-term organization-public relationships built and maintained? The literature offers some insights into ways for building and maintaining organization-public relationships.

**Strategies for Building and Maintaining
Organization-Public Relationships**

Recommendations for building and maintaining positive organization-public relationships vary from the general to the specific. Regardless of the degree of specificity they devote to the issue, organization-public relationship scholars agree on the importance of communication in the process of building and maintaining relationships. Broom et al. (1997) stated that relationships are formed and maintained through mutual adaptation and interactions aimed at attaining mutual goals. The communication linkage defines the relationship and the quality of the relationship itself can be assessed by looking at characteristics of the interactions between the organization and its publics.

Ledingham and Bruning (2000) and Ledingham (2003, 2006) argued that strategic communication programs can play a major role in building organization-public relationships. Managed communication programs that explain what an organization has done for the community and address the five relationship dimensions—openness, trust, involvement, investment, and commitment—can make a difference in the public's perception of the relationship with an organization.

J. E. Grunig and Huang (2000) showed how a number of specific interpersonal relationship maintenance and conflict resolution strategies can be used in public relations. Among relationship maintenance strategies, they discussed disclosure (being open, sharing information), giving the other party assurances of legitimacy, participating in common networks, and sharing tasks. One of the main questions this project seeks to answer is how these strategies are implemented on public relations Web sites. Web sites have been shown to play an important role in public relations, as the following section shows.

The Role of Web Sites in Organization-Public Relationship Building

Both scholars and practitioners of public relations feel that organizational Web sites play an important role in building and maintaining dialogue and relationships with important publics (Coombs, 1998; Hallahan, 2003; Heath, 1998; Kent & Tay'or, 1998), and increasing positive perceptions and loyalty towards an organization (Goldie, 2003; Hurst & Gellady, 1999, Newsome, Hill & White, 2000; Nielsen, 1997; Nielsen & Norman, 2000; White & Raman, 2000).

Kent and Taylor (1998) argued that Web sites can be used to create and maintain relationships between organizations and their publics and proposed principles for Web site design that facilitate dialogic organization-public relationships. Heath (1998) and Coombs (1998) saw in Web sites the potential to democratize discussions over social issues by making information and communication avenues available to activist groups, which have historically been at a disadvantage in their relationships with corporations. Hallahan (2003) made an argument for relationship building using Web sites and applied the model of organization-public relationships to Web sites, discussing antecedents, the process, and consequences of interacting with organizational Web sites.

In the professional world, there is also agreement that corporate public relations Web sites influence a public's perceptions of an organization, and loyalty towards it. Goldie (2003), Hurst and Gellady (1999), Nielsen (1997), and Nielsen and Norman (2000)

stated that providing a positive experience on the organization's Web site is crucial to maintaining a good relationship with publics, increasing reputation and customer loyalty, and ultimately surviving as a business. Interviews with public relations practitioners have shown they also feel that the public relations Web site contributes to the organization's reputation and so it is very important to have an up-to-date, competitive Web site (M. A. Johnson, 1997; Newland Hill & White, 2000; White & Raman, 2000).

The aforementioned arguments about a Web site's important role in building and maintaining organization-public relationships are supported by experimental studies showing that organizational Web sites influence perceptions of the relationship a public has with an organization, of corporate credibility and goodwill, and identification with the corporation (Jo & Kim, 2003; Len-Rios, 2003). However, the public relations Web site research does not provide insights into the process of interacting with the Web site, and the nature of a Web site experience that builds and maintains relationships—one of the voids in the literature that this study seeks to fill.

CHAPTER SUMMARY

The literature reviewed here provides insights about Web sites as rich communication environments, about the elements of Web site design, communication studies of Web sites, and organization-public relationships. The history and technologies of the World Wide Web have shaped the major values of Web-based communication: interconnectedness, open access, ease of use, and information sharing. The nature of Web communication is different from traditional media—with authors having more rhetorical choices but less authority, texts being nonlinear, decentralized, and open, and readers being actively involved and immersed in the communication experience. The literature also shows that this Web communication experience is fast, interactive, and often disorienting. These insights lead to the conclusion that the Web is a rich communication environment, and as such is the site of powerful communication experiences. Research has illuminated bits and pieces of this experience; however, no holistic and systematic framework for understanding and analyzing the communication Web site experience exists. The present project seeks to address this gap in the context of public relations.

A first step towards creating a framework of the public relations Web site experience is mapping the Web site space in which this experience takes place and understanding its constitutive elements. The Web design literature provides information about the building blocks of Web sites: verbal, visual, and multimedia content, layout, typography, links, and other organizational elements. The challenge is to organize these constitutive elements of Web sites in a systematic and coherent framework of the Web site space. Such a systematic framework could not be found in the literature about Web site studies. Moreover, communication and public relations studies of Web sites focus on analyzing the Web site content and ignore the communication experience as lived by the Web site visitor, so they cannot meaningfully explain either the human dimension of Web site use or the question of how relationships are formed in the process.

The last body of literature reviewed here offers useful insights about building, maintaining, and assessing relationships between organizations and their publics. The framework proposed in this research project merges these insights with the Web site user experience in order to conceptualize the public relations Web site experience: the experience of visiting a Web site that attempts to build and maintain positive relationships between organizations and publics. This framework is the subject of the following chapter.

CHAPTER 3

A FRAMEWORK
OF THE PUBLIC RELATIONS
WEB SITE EXPERIENCE

Creating a framework of the public relations Web site experience requires a set of fundamental dimensions for organizing the numerous aspects of this experience. It was established previously that the business and Web site design literature consider user perceptions, cognitions, attitudes and behaviors, as well as Web site aspects parts of the Web site user experience. An efficient framework needs to encompass all of these elements. The question becomes: What fundamental organizing dimensions can be used to provide the framework's basic structure?

The two fundamental dimensions that organize human experience are, according to Kant, time and space (Kant, 1787/2003; Scruton, 2001). Kant labeled time and space a priori intuitions and argued that they organize human perception and experience. Time and space are fundamental conditions of human sensibility that humans cannot escape: Human perception and experience outside time and space are not possible. Time and space can be understood as internal senses that humans project onto external reality. In this process, the perception of external reality is organized along the dimensions of time and space and so these dimensions provide the fundamental structure of our experience in the world.

The experience of visiting a Web site is a particular case of human experience and therefore the same organizing dimensions apply. Therefore, time and space are the two dimensions that provide the fundamental structure of the framework proposed here. The multiple elements of the Web site user experience can be organized along these two dimensions.

The temporal dimension of the Web site user experience consists of the sequence of perceptions, cognitions, attitudes, and behaviors that users go through as they visit a Web site. The spatial dimension is the Web site itself. The Web site provides a virtual space in which the user experience takes place. Fish (1980) briefly referred to text as spatial and the experience of reading as temporal. The framework proposed here echoes this idea, but does away with the separation between text and experience. In the present conceptualization, space (Fish's text) is a dimension of the Web site user experience, as opposed to being external to it. This is because the spatial and temporal dimensions are so closely interlinked that they cannot be perceived separately. After all, without a Web site to visit (spatial dimension), the user experience would not exist.

So both space and time are considered here equally important and fundamental organizing dimensions of the Web site user experience. This view allows for the proposition of the following definition:

> The Web site user experience is the sequence of perceptions, cognitions, attitudes and behaviors experienced by users in response to, and interaction with, the Web site's constitutive elements.

The remainder of this chapter provides detailed descriptions of the two dimensions of the Web site user experience. The major challenge, however, is not to describe these dimensions, but to understand how they are interlinked. In other words, the major question is: What Web site elements (spatial dimension) play major roles at what points during the Web site visit (temporal dimension)?

In the context of public relations, this question translates into the following: What Web site elements play important roles in creating/maintaining relationships with publics at what points of the Web site visit?

The following sections explain the spatial and temporal dimensions of the public relations Web site experience and propose research questions that explore the connections between the two dimensions. The order in which the dimensions are presented is not in any way indicative of their relative importance. Both the temporal and the spatial dimensions are equally important and interdependent.

THE SPATIAL DIMENSION

The spatial dimension of the Web site experience is the Web site itself, viewed as the virtual space in which the public relations

Web site experience takes place. The spatial dimension encompasses the various elements that compose a Web site. This section proposes a structure of the Web site virtual space.

Various authors list different components of Web sites, such as text, graphics, audio/video elements, navigation and interactivity (Brinck et al., 2002; Landow, 1997; Lemke, 2002; Nielsen, 2000a). As the technology advances, the list of possible Web site components will go on. Understanding Web sites requires understanding the elements that constitute them and their rhetorical potential, but compiling long lists might be less useful than proposing a framework capable of describing the overall structure of Web sites. Here Lev Manovich's (2001) thinking is of great help. Manovich listed modularity among the defining principles of new computer media. He pointed out that in new computer media, discrete objects are stored separately in the machine's memory, can be combined at will, and can be individually modified without necessarily changing the total product of which they are a part.

This modular view can be applied to Web sites in order to better understand their structure. Web sites can be broken down into four major layers: navigation, content, graphic layout, and dialogue. These layers can be conceived of as separate modules that are assembled and combined to form Web sites. Just like in Manovich's (2001) conceptualization, one Web site module can be changed without altering the others. For example, the graphic layout of a page can be changed while keeping the content the same—similar to a Microsoft PowerPoint presentation where one can change the graphic theme of a slide series without altering the content. Similarly, a different navigation scheme can be implemented on a Web site while keeping the content and graphic layout unchanged.

Web Site Modules
Content, navigation, graphic layout, and dialogue were proposed as the four overlapping layers that constitute Web sites. This section explains in more detail each type of module.

Content
The content module is hardly in need of explanation. It consists of various Web site elements with information value. Press releases, mission statements, photographs, and so forth, are all examples of Web site elements that make up the content module. Despite the popular adage that on the Web "content is king," the interaction among different Web site modules is probably more important than content alone. Prominence-interpretation theory (Fogg, 2003) explained that the quality content of a Web site does not matter much if the navigation scheme is so confusing that users cannot find that content in the first place.

Navigation
The navigation module helps users move through information space and maintain a sense of orientation. This module, referred to as the navigation scheme in professional Web design literature, is "embodied by graphical or textual aids including hypertext links, arrows, [site] maps, and icons" (Morville, 1996).

Graphic Layout
This module uses predominantly graphic elements with an organizational function to create the visual layout and hierarchy of the page. The goal of the graphic module is not just aesthetics. Rather, graphic design facilitates access to the content (Nielsen, 2000a)—it helps manage how users interact with information by structuring content and emphasizing important content elements

(Brinck et al., 2002). Typographic choices about font type, size, and color are also part of the graphic layout module.

Dialogic Module

The dialogic module consists of elements that allow users to engage in communication with the organization sponsoring the site. E-mail links, feedback forms, online surveys, and chat rooms are examples of elements constituting the dialogic module. This module facilitates two-way communication, which is a prerequisite of dialogue and of relationships between site users and authors/organizations (Kent & Taylor, 1998).

The Web Site Metaphor

Web site modules are graphically and conceptually held together by an overall theme or visual metaphor of the site. In the field of graphic interface design, metaphors are defined as conceptual schemes that rely on familiar objects and environments to facilitate users' understanding of a graphic interface (Laurel, 1991). The classic example of a metaphor is the computer desktop that uses the familiar objects of files, folders, trash cans, and so forth, to facilitate file management. Users intuit the function of the trash can icon on their screen based on their knowledge of trash cans in real life. Similarly, e-commerce sites use the metaphor of the shopping cart. Many Web sites use a general metaphor to organize their content: such as that of a shop, a library, a tree, a house, a ticket counter, and so forth, but metaphors can also be abstract and used just to provide visual unity and consistency to the different pages on a Web site (Nielsen, 2000a).

Modules are relatively large parts of Web sites and should not be confused with basic constitutive elements such as images, text, or links. A module may be a combination of any of these basic constitutive elements. For example, the navigation scheme of a Web site may consist of words, images, a sitemap, and other elements. An analogy with a building might be useful in explaining the distinction between Web site elements and modules. Examples of basic elements out of which a house is built are bricks, mortar, pipes and wires. An example of a module would be the electrical system that runs throughout the building and is made up of various basic elements. The question becomes: What elements are the bricks and mortar of Web sites? What are the raw materials out of which Web sites can be created? An inventory of elements discussed in various Web design manuals points to four basic types of Web site elements: text, graphics, audio, and video.

So far, I have proposed a modular structure of the Web site space composed of four types of modules. In turn, each module can be constituted by a combination of any of four types of basic elements: text, graphics, audio, and video. However, this conceptualization does not exhaust the complexity of Web sites. It fails to explain why a certain element (i.e., an image) belongs to a module. For example, an image can be a link and belong to the navigation module, but at the same time it can have information value which would place it in the content module. So any given element can have one or more functions on a Web site, and it is the function that determines what module the element belongs to. The following section explains element functions.

Element Functions

In his book on the culture of graphic interfaces, Johnson (1997) stated that text can be encountered on the computer screen as content, or as command—for example, a link. Lemke (2002) proposed a framework for hypertext in which each type of sign (image or text) could make three types of meaning: presentational, orientational, and organizational. By presentational

meaning, Lemke referred to content per se, the presentation of
a state of affairs. Orientational meaning designates what communication scholars name metacommunication: communication
about the process of communication itself, and about the relationship and stances of the interactants. Organizational meaning
signals how the text is organized, which parts come together in
structural units, and what the relationships between parts are.
Drawing on Johnson (1997) and Lemke (2002), I propose that
on a Web site, an individual element can have one or more of the
following four possible functions:

Symbolic

The element has informational content. This function is an exten-
sion of Lemke's presentational function. The element presents a
state of affairs, a position, an argument, and so forth. One example of an element with the presentational function is a paragraph
of text. Another example can be a color scheme that uses symbolic colors. For example, www.moveon.org, a site that mobilizes
online activists uses red, white, and blue for its color scheme.

Command

The element is the trigger of an (inter)action. Interacting with
the module will trigger an action or a change. Links, buttons,
and search boxes are examples of elements with the command
function. The command function is the manifestation of a Web
site's interactivity. The way the command function is implemented on a Web site determines how interactive the Web site is.
Interactivity has been conceptualized as a variable on a contin-
uum (Rafaeli, 1988; Sims, 1997), and so Web site elements such
as links are examples of relatively low interactivity, whereas
elements that allow users to manipulate variables and observe
the outcomes in real time are highly interactive. An example of

elements with command functions that exhibit high interactivity are online auto payment calculators that allow users to enter variables such as interest rates and length of loans to see how the total loan amount or the monthly payment change as a function of the other variables.

Organizational
This element contributes to the graphic or conceptual structuring of the Web site environment. Graphic markers of sections and subsections, column separators, and headings and subheadings are examples of elements with the organizational function.

Metacommunication
This element contains overt or subtle messages about the nature of the relationship and of the interaction between the Web site's authors and users. This function is similar to Lemke's (2002) understanding of orientational meaning and includes content and design choices that are perceived as restrictive, rude, or on the contrary, friendly and polite. For example, a Web site's navigation solution can be perceived as rude and restrictive if it does not allow visitors the freedom to view pages in any order they prefer. Linear navigation that forces visitors to go through pages one at a time, in the order determined by the Web site author, can be perceived as a statement about the inability of the Web site visitor to make the right decisions when navigating the Web site. Word choices can also provide hints about the perceived or intended relationship between an organization and its Web site visitors.

It could be argued that a fifth possible function of Web site elements exists—a purely aesthetic one. I believe, however, that aesthetics in the context of Web site elements is better conceived of as a quality that the elements can have and may be judged upon, rather than a function.

Any particular element of a Web site module can manifest one or more of the aforementioned four functions. For example, a text element can be a heading (organizational function) and at the same time a link (command function). The word choices in the heading may also indicate a metacommunication function.

This section has proposed a modular view of the Web site virtual space. The structure of the Web site virtual space can be seen as a combination of four major modules: content, navigation, graphic layout, and dialogic. The modules are constituted of any of the four basic Web site elements: verbal discourse, graphics, audio, and video. Each Web site element can have one or more of four functions: symbolic, command, organizational, and metacommunication. An element's functions determine what module(s) it belongs to. This section has only dealt with components of the Web site virtual space. The dialogic module, for example, only refers to Web site elements (such as feedback forms, forums, chat rooms, etc.), that make dialogue possible and does not in any way imply or guarantee that dialogue actually happens during the Web site experience. Similarly, the navigation module refers to Web site elements such as links and menus, not to a Web site's visitor experience of navigating the Web site. Although the navigation module is likely to play a major role in the Web site visitors' navigation experience, the two are different. The navigation module refers to Web site features, whereas the act of navigating refers to the user's actions, perceptions, decisions, and so forth. The sequence of user perceptions, cognitions, and behaviors are described along the temporal dimension of the Web site experience.

THE TEMPORAL DIMENSION

The temporal dimension of the Web site experience was defined earlier as the sequence of perceptions, cognitions, and behaviors that users go through as they visit a Web site's virtual space. The temporal dimension can be described as having three main consecutive phases: phase one, of first impressions; phase two, of Web site exploration; and phase three, exit. The first and last phases of the Web site experience are likely to be much shorter than the exploration phase. However, each phase is an important part of the Web site experience. The three phases and the steps that constitute them are described next.

Phase One: First Impression
Research shows it takes Web site users a very short time to decide whether to stay on a site or to continue their search for information elsewhere (Nielsen, 2001c; Nielsen & Tahir, 2002). In the first few seconds of exposure to a Web site's homepage, users form expectations about the relevance and the quality of information available on that Web site. The question "Is this what I am looking for?" is answered by users quickly, and depending upon the probability of the answer being "yes," a decision is made whether to continue exploring the Web site or not. From a public relations perspective, this decision is very important. If the visitor decides to leave the Web site immediately, the opportunity to engage in relationship work is missed. This is why it is important for the public relations Web site to create a positive first impression that will entice visitors to stay.

Empirical research is needed, and is undertaken in this project, to establish what Web site elements users base their initial impressions on. What we know about human perception of printed pages indicates that at first the homepage is perceived as a blurry whole, and then vision focuses in on specific elements, as guided by the graphic design of that page (Faiola, 2000). Some usability studies have found that users first look at the content area, and only later at navigation and graphics when they scan a new page (Nielsen, 2000d). Credibility research has found that people often base their overall evaluation of Web sites on the graphic design (Fogg, Marable et al., 2002). These controversial research findings show that it is still not clear what elements of Web sites influence first impressions and the initial decision to stay on the site. Which elements contribute to the formation of expectations about the Web site has to be determined through more research with users.

If, following the first phase, the user makes the decision to exit, the Web site experience skips the middle phase and ends. If a decision is made to stay, the user will move on to the second phase, exploration.

Phase Two: Exploration

Once the user has decided to stay on the site, he or she has to find the desired information. Usability research has shown that a first step in this phase is that of orientation, during which the user learns about the Web site. Usability experts have concluded that every Web site is a learning experience (Nielsen, 2000a). This is the main reason why usability experts recommend following widely accepted design standards, so that users will not have to learn each Web site all over, and will be able to rely on previous knowledge. What needs to be learned about a Web site during the orientation step? One main part that usability experts point out is the navigation solution, or how to navigate the Web site. Although the practice of linking is common to all Web sites, links can be implemented in many ways. Users have to learn what elements of the site are links and how they work (by clicking, placing the mouse over the link, through drop-down menus, etc.) in order to be able to use the Web site (Nielsen, 2000a). The second thing that users probably gain during the orientation step is a general sense of where to find information on the site by forming a rudimentary mental map or model of the site. There is much discussion among Web site usability researchers about the formation of mental models of sites (Brinck et al., 2002; Spool, 1999), but there is enough evidence to suggest that some, if not all users, form at least a rudimentary mental map of the site that helps them maintain orientation in the information space. Therefore, at this point of the temporal dimension, it can be proposed that the first step of the exploration phase is *orientation*, during which users learn how the Web site works and form a mental map of the site. Usability research suggests that during the orientation step, the navigation module is likely to play an important role in the Web site experience.

Orientation is a necessary preliminary phase of relationship building. If Web site visitors do not manage to learn how to use the Web site, or are frustrated and disoriented, they might not engage the Web site further, or might perceive the Web site and the organization it represents negatively.

Following the orientation step, users engage the navigation and content parts of the Web site in what can be labeled the *engagement* step. As discussed in the literature review, usability research has proposed several models of how people navigate Web sites (Brinck et al., 2002; Eveland & Dunwoody, 1998). At this step of the experience, users engage in information learning and evaluation, while at the same time trying to maintain their orientation within the Web site (Eveland & Dunwoody, 1998, 2000). The engagement step presents the most opportunities for relationship work on a Web site. This is why public relations Web sites attempt to conserve visitors by keeping them on the site as much as possible (Kent & Taylor, 1998). Building "sticky sites," as Web designers call them, is a major goal (Hammerich & Harrison, 2001; Kent & Taylor, 1998; Kyrnin, 2004; Nielsen, 2000a; Powell, 2002). As long as visitors are exploring the Web site, there is a possibility to engage them in a relationship with the organization the Web site represents. The engagement step of the public relations Web site experience, therefore, is characterized by two major aspects: visitor conservation and relationship building/maintenance work.

So far, it has been proposed that the second phase of the Web site experience, exploration, consists of two steps: the orientation step during which users learn the Web site, and the engagement step during which users actively engage the navigation and content aspects. At some point, users will leave the Web site, thus initiating the third and last phase of the Web site visit, the exit.

Phase Three: Exit

Users may exit a Web site in an accidental or intentional way. Accidental exits may happen when a user follows a link which is not clearly labeled as outgoing and leads to a page on a different site (Brinck et al., 2002). Intentional exiting involves making the decision to leave the site. Users may leave the site because they decided it did not contain the information they were looking for, because they found the required information and decided to close the session, or because they were frustrated and dissatisfied (Nielsen, 1999a, 2000a). The reasons why people leave Web sites are explained by usability research. The lasting impressions that are formed by the time of exit are more important than the reasons why people leave. By the exit phase, users have probably formed an overall evaluation of the site and have made a decision whether to return to that specific site in the future (Kent & Taylor, 1998; Nielsen, 2000a). An important empirical question to ask about the Web site experience is what aspects users base these decisions upon.

This section has proposed a description of the temporal dimension of the public relations Web site experience. Three phases of the Web site experience have been described: first impression, exploration (with the orientation and engagement steps), and exit. The existence of these phases is suggested and supported by results of Web site usability and user behavior research.

So far, the spatial and the temporal dimensions of the Web site user experience have been described. Research is needed to connect the temporal and the spatial dimensions. It might be possible that at certain phases of the experience, a certain module, or element function, is predominant. For example, the literature suggests that the navigation module plays a central role during the orientation step of the Web site experience. But does it play a role in establishing trust? What Web site elements or modules are influential in creating relationships with visitors? Do Web site visitors consistently look to a certain part of the Web site when making specific decisions? What module influences the visitors' first impression or the decision to stay on the Web site? These are questions to be answered in this research project.

The following section proposes a series of research questions that explore the connections between the temporal and the spatial dimensions of the public relations Web site experience. It is important to bear in mind that the connections might vary for different interpretive communities, or publics. For example, during the first impression phase, one public might focus on graphic elements, whereas another might pay more attention to headings and titles. So, in the first impression phase, the first public's Web site experience will display a connection with the graphic module and the second public's, a connection with the content module. The same list of research questions and the corresponding questionnaire items described in chapter 4 can be used to map out the Web site experiences of various communities. Caution is needed, however, when attempting to generalize results across publics.

RESEARCH QUESTIONS

In order to identify connections between the spatial and the temporal dimensions of the public relations Web site experience, the research questions need to be anchored in one of the dimensions and ask about the corresponding aspects of the other dimension. One possibility is to anchor the research questions in the spatial dimension. Each question could inquire about each spatial component's connection with phases of the temporal dimension. For example, a research question could ask: During what phases of the temporal experience does the content module play important roles? Another possibility is to anchor the research questions in the temporal dimension and ask what spatial aspects play predominant roles during each phase. For example, a research question could ask: What Web site aspects play important roles during the first impression phase?

The structure of the dimension in which the questions are anchored determines the organization of the research questions. Because the spatial dimension has a complex, modular structure, and the temporal dimension has a simple linear structure, the latter is used in this project to anchor the research questions. So, each of the following research questions explores connections between a phase or step of the temporal dimension and aspects of the spatial dimension.

The first phase of the temporal dimension is the first impression. The following question explores the connections between this phase and the spatial dimension:

> **Research Question 1:** *What elements is the Web site visitors' first impression based upon?*

The second phase of the temporal dimension, exploration, has two steps: orientation and engagement. In order to connect the orientation step of the temporal dimension with the spatial dimension, the following research questions are advanced:

Research Question 2: *What Web site elements, if any, help visitors stay oriented on the Web site?*

Research Question 3: *What Web site elements, if any, do visitors find confusing and disorienting?*

The engagement step, as was established in the description of the temporal dimension, is characterized by the conservation of Web site visitors through maintaining their interest, and engaging in relationship building and maintenance. These two aspects prompt the following research questions:

Research Question 4: *What Web site elements, if any, keep visitors from leaving the Web site?*

Research Question 5: *What Web site elements, if any, contribute to the visitors' perceptions that they are invited to engage in a relationship with the organization the Web site represents?*

The public relations literature shows that the relationship concept is complex and multidimensional. A single research question is not sufficient for addressing the complexities of the relationship concept. Different research questions are needed for each relevant dimension of the organization-public relationship. As shown in the literature review, different relationship measurement scales assess different relationship dimensions. However, the dimensions of trust, commitment, and involvement are common to the scales proposed by Bruning and Ledingham (Bruning, 2002; Bruning & Ledingham, 1998, 1999, 2000; Ledingham & Bruning, 1998, 2000), J. E. Grunig and colleagues (J. E. Grunig, 2002; J. E. Grunig & Huang, 2000; Hon &

J. E. Grunig, 1999), Huang (2001), and Kim (2001). Perceptions of trust, commitment, and involvement have been established as valid and reliable indicators of a positive organization-public relationship. In addition, openness and dialogue are two important dimensions of relationship building (Bruning & Ledingham, 1999; J. E. Grunig & Huang; Kent & Taylor, 1998; Kent et al., 2003; Ledingham, 2003; Ledingham & Bruning, 1998, 2000) that are particularly relevant to the Web site context. Openness is directly related to public relations Web sites because sharing information is one of the main purposes of having a Web site in the first place. It is important to assess what Web site elements contribute to the visitors' perceptions of organizational openness. In this day and age when most U.S. corporations have a Web site, the fact of having a Web site itself cannot be automatically interpreted as a sign of openness. Organizations might have Web sites, yet not be open about sharing information on them; or try to be open, but not be perceived as such because of design and technical errors. This is why the dimension of openness needs to be included in the present research.

Finally, dialogue has been shown to be a central dimension of organization-public relationships (Kent & Taylor, 1998, 2002) and is particularly relevant to public relations Web sites. Web sites are suited for dialogue because the technology allows for two-way communication. Two-way communication is an essential part of excellent public relations (J. E. Grunig & Hunt, 1984; J. E. Grunig & IABC Research Foundation., 1992; L. A. Grunig et al., 2002) and a prerequisite for establishing genuine dialogue between organizations and their publics (Kent & Taylor). The extent to which organizations take advantage of the technology and express an interest in listening to publics varies. Because public relations Web sites already are the voices of organizations, an interest to engage in two-way communication and even dialogue is indicated online by willingness or invitations to listen to visitors. This project inquires what Web site aspects are interpreted by visitors as signs of organizational interest in two-way communication and dialogue. The organization-public relationship dimension of dialogue should not be confused with the dialogic module of the spatial dimension. Although it is possible that the dialogic module (Web site elements that facilitate two-way communication) will play an important role in Web site visitors' perceptions that the organization is interested in engaging in dialogue with them, the two similar terms refer to different phenomena.

In sum, in order to assess relationship work on Web sites, it is important to address Web site visitors' perceptions of the relationship dimensions of trust, commitment, involvement, openness, and dialogue. In order to connect these perceptions with the spatial dimension and to identify what Web site elements contribute to their formation, the following questions are proposed:

Research Question 5a: *What Web site elements, if any, contribute to visitors' perceptions that they can trust the organization the Web site represents?* (dimension of trust)

Research Question 5b: *What Web site elements, if any, contribute to visitors' perceptions that the organization is interested in maintaining a relationship with them?* (dimension of commitment)

Research Question 5c: *What Web site elements, if any, contribute to the visitors' perceptions that the organization is involved in helping the community?* (dimension of involvement)

Research Question 5d: *What Web site elements, if any, contribute to the Web site visitors' perceptions that the organization is open about sharing information?* (dimension of openness)

> **Research Question 5e:** *What Web site elements, if any, contribute to the Web site visitors' perceptions that the organization is interested in listening to them?* (dimension of dialogue)

The exploration phase is followed by the exit phase. Web site usability and online user behavior research has already established the reasons why visitors leave Web sites, so a research question exploring these reasons is not needed. Besides, the research protocol used in this project (described in chapter 4) instructs participants to leave the Web sites when they feel they are ready to answer a series of questions about them, so in this situation, the reason for leaving is already known. However, research questions are needed to address other important aspects of the exit phase, namely the visitors' overall opinions of the Web site, and intention to return.

> **Research Question 6:** *What Web site elements contribute to the visitors' overall evaluation of the Web site?*

> **Research Question 7:** *What Web site elements, if any, contribute to visitors' decision to return to the Web site?*

This section has advanced research questions about the connections of each phase of the temporal dimension with aspects of the Web site virtual space. The research questions aim to identify what Web site aspects visitors focus on at different phases of the Web site experience, and what Web site aspects are perceived to be relevant to the relationship dimensions of trust, commitment, involvement, openness, and dialogue.

CHAPTER SUMMARY

So far, I have discussed the two dimensions of the public relations Web site experience and proposed research questions to explore the connections between the two dimensions. The spatial dimension is the virtual space of the Web site itself. This space has been explained as being constituted by combinations of modules, which in turn are made up of elements. Elements are the smallest constitutive unit of a Web site and can have one or more of four possible functions: symbolic, command, organizational, and metacommunication. Element functions determine what modules elements belong to: content, navigation, graphic design, and/or the dialogic module. The temporal dimension consists of the sequence of perceptions, cognitions, and behaviors the user experiences during the Web site visit and can be broken into three main phases: first impression, exploration, and exit.

The last part of this chapter has proposed a series of research questions that explore the connection between the spatial and the temporal dimensions of the public relations Web site experience. For the sake of clear organization, the research questions were anchored in the temporal dimension. Research questions were proposed for each phase and step of the temporal dimension. Each question asked what Web site aspects (spatial dimension) play predominant roles during each phase or step (temporal dimension). Anchoring the research questions in the temporal dimension is not an indication that the temporal aspects are more important than the spatial ones. As explained before, the research questions could have been anchored in the spatial dimension and could have asked during what phase or step each module, element, and element function plays an important role. The advantage of anchoring the research questions in the temporal dimension is the simple linear organization of the research questions that followed from the structure of the temporal dimension.

The next chapter explains the research undertaken in order to answer the research questions and describes the research methods.

CHAPTER 4

METHODS

The purpose of conducting empirical research for this project was to answer the twelve research questions exploring the connections between the temporal and the spatial dimensions of the public relations Web site experience. The research questions asked what Web site elements (spatial dimension) shape each phase of the Web site visit (temporal dimension).

The interface design industry has conducted research about the experience of using software and Web sites for a while now. However, most of this research focused on usability. Usability research is primarily concerned with the ease of use and the ease of learning a Web site (Nielsen, 2000a). The main purpose of usability research is to identify problems users encounter as they try to accomplish tasks. The purpose of this project, however, is not to test the usability of Web sites, but to understand the connections between the spatial and temporal dimensions of the public relations

Web site experience. A Web site's usability is part of the public relations Web site experience and can influence it to a great extent. This is why it is important to take usability into consideration when analyzing the public relations Web site experience. However, the public relations Web site experience encompasses much more than usability. This research aims to identify how organization-public relationships are created and maintained online. Because the purpose of this research is different from Web site usability, usability research methods were modified to create a new research protocol—Web site experience analysis.

Web site experience analysis borrows from usability research only the general research setting. That is, just like in usability testing, research participants are invited one by one to browse a Web site and to answer questions about it. Beyond the general research setting, Web site experience analysis is different from usability research in at least three important ways.

The first main difference between Web site experience analysis and usability research concerns the measures. The main measures of usability testing are related to task performance, and evaluation questionnaires are only secondary. However, as opposed to usability testing, Web site experience analysis is not concerned with participants' task performance, but with the attitudes and interpretations participants create during the Web site experience. For this research, task performance cannot provide in-depth information about the Web user experience. Detailed evaluations and accounts of each phase of the Web site visit are needed. This is the reason why the main assessment tool is a questionnaire inquiring about the phases of the Web site visit and Web site elements.

The second important difference between Web site experience analysis and usability research is the research protocol. In usability research, participants are provided with a series of specific information retrieval, evaluation, and comparison tasks to perform. In Web site experience analysis, the participants' only task is to examine the Web site and try to form an opinion of it. The reason for asking research participants to evaluate the Web site is to avoid the time pressure associated with task performance and to allow for unhurried inspection of the Web site, which mimics leisure browsing.

The third difference between the two types of research concerns the choice of Web sites to analyze. In usability testing, it is usually clear what Web site(s) need to be tested. Here, a sample of corporate public relations Web sites has to be selected.

The Web site experience analysis research protocol is described next, followed by an explanation of Web site sample selection, research participant recruitment, and the construction of the questionnaire.

WEB SITE EXPERIENCE ANALYSIS

The Web site experience analysis research protocol used in this study asked participants to examine a Web site and answer a series of questions about it. Just like usability testing, Web site experience analysis was conducted with one research participant at a time. This section first describes the physical setting in which data collection took place, then the procedures used with each research participant.

Physical Setting

Data collection was conducted in a quiet group collaboration room located in a digital learning laboratory. Two notebook computers were set up side by side for research participants. One computer was used for administering a computer-based questionnaire and the other for visiting a preselected corporate Web site. The researcher was present in the room during data collection. However, the researcher did not closely observe the participants' behaviors and did not have visual access to the participants' computer screens.

Procedures

Upon arrival to the collaboration room, participants were greeted and asked to read and sign the informed consent forms approved by the Institutional Review Board at Purdue University (Appendix A). They were informed that participation was voluntary, and that the researcher would strive to keep their identity confidential.

Upon agreeing to participate in the research, the participants were given a brief overview of the research protocol. Participants were told that their task was to evaluate the Web site and were asked to browse it in order to form an opinion of it. The computer-based questionnaire contained more detailed instructions about the procedures to be followed by participants. After receiving an overview of the procedures, participants were asked whether they had any questions, and after clearing any potential issues, they were invited to start by answering a series of background questions on the first computer. The last background question was followed by instructions for participants to turn to the second computer and begin browsing the Web site.

In order to avoid premature exposure to the Web site to be evaluated, a splash page containing only the word *start* was created and displayed on the second computer. Upon clicking the link, the research participants were able to see the homepage of the actual Web site. The time elapsed between the click of the link on the splash page and the moment of the first click off the Web site's homepage was operationalized as the duration of forming a first impression and was noted. At the moment of the first click off the Web site's homepage, the researcher interrupted participants and asked them to answer a series of questions about participants' first impression of the Web site. At the end of the series, the questionnaire displayed instructions to continue browsing the Web site and return to the first computer when the participants felt they have formed an opinion of the site. Participants continued browsing the Web site and, whenever ready, they finished the questionnaire and submitted the answers. Before leaving the room, the participants were given a chance to ask questions about the research and the uses of the data collected.

The cookies and temporary Internet files were cleared after each Web site visit to ensure that all participants' experiences were similar. Dynamic, data-driven Web sites have the capacity to adapt themselves to subsequent visits based on the information collected about the user during previous Web site usage. By clearing the cookies and the temporary Internet files, the researcher could make sure that each participant was treated like a first-time visitor to each Web site.

This section has described the Web site experience analysis research protocol employed to collect data for this project. The next section explains how the Web sites participants looked at were selected.

WEB SITE SELECTION

Chapter 1 explained that the scope of this research was limited to Web sites of U.S. corporations. Considering the number of corporate Web sites on the WWW, it is impossible to select a random sample. Besides, a random sample would not have been the most appropriate for this research. Given the exploratory nature of this research, in-depth qualitative data about a small, purposive sample (Patton, 2002) of corporate Web sites can provide more insight into the public relations Web site experience than a study of a large representative random sample. Moreover, since this research inquired about online relationship building, it was important to select Web sites that participants were not familiar with, so their perceptions and evaluations would be in response to the Web site experience and not to prior experience with the corporation or its products. A random sample of corporate Web sites could not have ensured that research participants would be unfamiliar with the corporations, whereas a purposive sample could.

Because this type of research is new, there are no guidelines in the literature about the number of Web sites necessary for conducting a Web site experience analysis study. The qualitative and exploratory nature of this research did not require a large sample size, and corporate Web sites are similar enough so as not to require the inclusion of a large number of sites. Similar Web site studies have analyzed between 4 and 20 Web sites (Benoit & Benoit, 2000; Brunn & Cottle, 1997; Curtin & Gaither, 2003; Nielsen, 2001a, 2003a), so nine Web sites were considered sufficient to draw conclusions for this study.

In order to achieve some breadth, Web sites of different size corporations were selected from business ranking lists. Large corporations were selected from the 2004 Fortune 100 list (revenues ranging between $18,878.0–$258,681.0 million), medium corporations from the 2004 Fortune 900–1000 list ($1,188.4–$1,392.7 million in revenue), and small ones ($6.0–$196.9 million) from the 2003 Fortune Small Business 100 list, all available on the *Fortune* Web site. The researcher looked at each list and first excluded very well-known corporations. Then, corporations that were not likely to be of interest to members of the general consumer public, such as military contractors, or producers of high-end medical equipment, were also excluded. Then, the researcher selected about 10 corporations representing different industries from each list. Another list was compiled, containing these corporations' names and short descriptions of their business profiles. Undergraduate students were asked informally whether they were familiar with the corporations and whether they would be likely to visit their Web sites. Three large, three medium, and three small corporations' Web sites were chosen that students were not familiar with but they were likely to visit. The three large corporations' Web sites were Valero Energy (2004), Medco Health Solutions (2004), and Weyerhaeuser (2004). The medium corporations' Web sites were Westcorp (2004), Fred's (2004), and Equifax (2004); and the small corporations' Web sites were Virbac (2004), North Coast Energy (2004), and Horizon Organic (2004). These corporations' Web sites were easily identified using a search engine.

Having explained how the nine corporate Web sites for this study were selected, the next section discusses the selection and characteristics of the research participants.

RESEARCH PARTICIPANTS

In the absence of other guidelines for deciding the appropriate number of research participants, guidelines from usability research were used. Nielsen (2000e) argued that only five participants are needed to test a Web site's usability. Beyond five, the results become repetitive. Preferring to err on the conservative side, this study collected data from 6 research participants for each of the nine Web sites, which brought the number of research participants to 54.

Research participants were recruited among students enrolled in an undergraduate communication class. Participation was voluntary and rewarded by a small number of extra credit points. The same number of extra credit points was available to students for an alternative assignment. This recruiting procedure is often used at research universities to help undergraduate students become familiar with research methods in their field of study. The recruitment procedure was approved by the Institutional Review Board. Data was collected until six completed questionnaires were accumulated for each Web site. To compensate for six completed questionnaires lost because of technical errors, data was collected from sixty students.

Out of the 54 students whose answers were saved and analyzed in this study, 40 were female and 14 were male, with ages ranging between 19–25 years. The mean age of the research participants was 20. Most research participants were sophomores (36). Thirteen were juniors, 3 were seniors, and 2 were freshmen. Overall, the research participants had quite a lot of experience using computers ($M = 9.5$ years). They reported having used computers for 4–16 years. They all reported using computers frequently, at least once a day. The research participants' experience using the Internet was on average 6.7 years, ranging between 3 and 10 years and all but one reported going online at least once a day. Overall, the participants' attitudes towards computers were positive. Thirty-nine reported that they enjoy using computers very much, 12 answered somewhat, and only 3 were neutral.

A convenience student sample is usually considered a limitation, but in this case, it is an acceptable one. Undergraduate students are a valid public of U.S. corporations, and are likely to use corporate Web sites when researching products, company policies, and employment opportunities. Although other corporate Web site publics' experiences are likely to differ from those of students, the overall structure of the experience remains the same because the dimensions of time and space are universal. This study demonstrates how an interpretive community's public relations Web site experience is mapped out by ascertaining the connections between the spatial and the temporal dimensions. The purpose of this research is not to identify differences between interpretive communities, but to demonstrate how the framework is used to understand a public's Web site experience. Future studies could use the same framework to study other aspects of the Web site experience, including differences among interpretive communities, but for the purpose of this research, it is sufficient to study one public.

After describing the research protocol, Web site selection, and participant recruitment, the last part of this research methodology that needs to be explained is the questionnaire construction. The following section addresses this aspect.

QUESTIONNAIRE CONSTRUCTION

Usability testing requires the use of a background questionnaire to collect information about personal variables that might influence people's experiences with Web sites. This kind of background questionnaire asks participants for some demographic data and information about their experience and attitudes using computers and the Internet (Nielsen, 1993). A similar background questionnaire is used in Web site experience analysis. All questionnaires used in this research protocol, including the background questionnaire, were computer based. A list of the questions it contained is included in Appendix B.

After completing the background questionnaire, participants proceeded to the main questionnaire. The purpose of the main questionnaire was to identify connections between the spatial and the temporal dimensions of the Web site experience by answering the twelve research questions. At least one pair of items was used to collect data about each research question.

Because the research questions were anchored in the temporal dimension, they asked about the Web site aspects (spatial dimension) corresponding to each phase and step of the Web site experience. The questionnaire items followed the same pattern. For example, items asked what Web site aspects that played important roles during the first impression phase, the two steps of the exploration phase (orientation and engagement), and during the exit phase. As explained in chapter 3, relationship building and maintenance work is associated with the engagement step, so questions about the five organization-public relationship dimensions were asked after those about orientation but before those about exit.

The first item of each pair addressed the temporal dimension and asked participants to rate aspects of each phase of the Web site experience. For example, one item asked them to rate their first impression of the Web site. The first item in a pair was closed-ended, asking participants to rate their opinions on a 10-point scale. The 10-point scale has the advantages that it is common and familiar, and more nuanced than the 5-point scale, which tends to produce only ratings of 2, 3, and 4 (Whitman, 2004). The more sensitive 10-point scale can be reduced to 5 categories after the data is collected.

The second item in each pair addressed the spatial dimension and asked participants to discuss the Web site aspects their opinion is based upon. Typically, the second items in each pair, all open-ended, were worded as follows: "What Web site aspects make you think so?"

The construction of the item pairs is consistent with prominence-interpretation theory (Fogg, 2003). Prominence-interpretation theory states that the credibility of a Web site element is a function of the element's prominence (whether it is noticed) and its interpretation by the Web site visitor. The questions were constructed so as not to direct the research participants' attention to certain Web site elements, thus missing out on the prominence aspect. The first item in each pair assessed interpretation at each phase of the Web site experience, and the second one assessed prominence by asking what Web site aspects the interpretation was based upon. A typical pair of items, addressing the relationship dimension of trust, is listed as follows:

> Do you feel you can trust this organization?
> (not at all) 1 2 3 4 5 6 7 8 9 10 (very much)
>
> What on the Web site makes you feel this way?

A list of all the questions included in the main questionnaire can be found in Appendix C. The items addressing the organization-public relationship dimensions of trust, commitment, involvement, and openness were adapted from items developed and used by Bruning and Ledingham (1998, 1999, 2000) and Ledingham and Bruning (1999, 2000).

CHAPTER SUMMARY

This chapter explained the research protocol used in this study. Drawing on usability research (Nielsen, 1993), a new research protocol—Web site experience analysis—was proposed and described. The chapter also explained how nine corporate Web sites were selected for inclusion in this study, and discussed the recruitment of research participants. The last section provided the rationale for building the questionnaires used in this study. The next chapter presents and discusses the study's results.

CHAPTER 5

RESULTS AND DISCUSSION

This chapter summarizes the analysis of data collected to answer the twelve research questions introduced in chapter 3. The chapter is structured in three main sections: The first provides a description of the procedures used for analyzing the data, the second presents the results, and the third discusses them.

DATA ANALYSIS

For all but one of the twelve research questions, the main questionnaire (see Appendix C) contained at least one pair of items. The first item in the pair asked participants to rate their opinions of various aspects of the Web site experience on a 10-point scale. The second item asked participants to describe what Web site aspects their opinion was based upon. So the first item in each pair produced ordinal-level quantitative data, and the second one, qualitative data. This section explains how the data were analyzed for the two types of items. The same analyses were repeated for each research question.

The data were first analyzed individually for each item, and then a connection was established between the two. For the quantitative items, frequency counts were first computed. The 10-point scale was collapsed into five categories by grouping 2 adjacent ratings in one category. Ratings of 1 and 2 were combined into a *negative* category, ratings of 3 and 4 into a *somewhat negative* category, and so on. The reason for using a 10-point scale and then collapsing it into five categories was to obtain a wider range of ratings. Research shows that subjects tend to avoid the extreme points of scales, so a 5-point scale is likely to produce only ratings of 2, 3, and 4 (Whitman, 2004). Using a 10-point scale that can later be clustered into five categories avoids this limitation of 5-point scales.

After computing the frequency counts of the ratings on the quantitative item, the median score for each of the nine Web sites included in this analysis was identified. The reason for reporting data for each Web site was to observe whether there were major differences among the nine Web sites. When major differences in median ratings are present, they are discussed in the results section by looking at the participants' comments about the Web sites with extreme ratings. For example, the median first impression scores show that Valero's Web site received the highest ratings, whereas Equifax received the lowest. The participants who visited Valero's Web site reported liking the images and the overall layout and visual appeal of the page, whereas those who visited Equifax commented about ambiguity, clutter, and the lack of visual focus. When no major differences are identified in the median ratings, the scores are not discussed in detail.

When calculating the median ratings, the 10-point scales were used as such. Collapsing them to 5 points would have resulted in very homogeneous median ratings that would have not provided much information about the differences among the nine Web sites. For example, if the median ratings had been computed from a 5-point scale, six out of the nine Web sites would have received the same rating, thus masking some differences.

For the qualitative items, the first step was to identify recurring themes in the answers provided. Then the main themes were summarized in a report. When reviewing the themes, it became obvious that the themes were present in the data with either a negative or a positive valence. So each occurrence of a main theme was coded as positive or negative. For example, a comment about the lack of visual focus was coded as negative, whereas one about the presence of visual focus (eye-catching elements) was coded as positive. Similarly, a comment about too much clutter on a page was coded as negative, whereas a comment that stated the page was not cluttered was coded as positive.

The polarity of comments is explained by the fact that the participants provided these comments to justify their evaluative opinions of various aspects of their Web site experience. While justifying their opinions, participants referred to Web site aspects they liked or disliked. For example, in the following description of a participant's first impression, seven themes were identified: professional, attractive, colors, pictures, links, cluttered, and ambiguous. The first five themes were coded as positive comments, and the last two as negative:

> Initially, I thought that the Web site looked cluttered. It looks professional with the pictures and icons, and so forth, but there are a lot of words in a relatively small space. The only part I had time to really read was the

small introduction under the large "Equifax." It was vague and didn't give me a good idea of what the company actually does. Aside from the cluttered appearance and vague description, the Web site looks good with several different colors and places to go.

Lastly, another report was produced that connected the quantitative and the qualitative items. This last report tabulates the main themes identified in the qualitative items within each of the five rating categories (negative, somewhat negative, neutral, somewhat positive, and positive). For example, for the first impression items, participants who rated their first impression as positive referred in their open-ended answers to the Web sites' pictures, visual appeal, colors, links and headings, organization, and so forth, whereas those who rated their first impression as somewhat negative referred to different themes, such as the lack of visual focus, ambiguity, and clutter.

Although 54 data sets were collected, some participants chose not to answer certain questions, which resulted in missing data. Missing data is indicated by a blank table cell in the following reports.

The next section presents the results of these analyses.

RESULTS

The results presented in this section are all based on data collected in a two-week period in March 2004. To optimize the presentation of the results and to avoid redundancy, the analyses were compiled into three reports. The first report summarizes the main themes identified in the qualitative answers. The second one presents frequency counts for each of the five rating categories, along with summaries of the main themes corresponding to each category. The third report lists each Web site's median rating. Similar reports are presented for each research question.

Research Question 1

The first research question asked what Web site elements the Web site visitors' first impression was based upon. The time it took participants to form a first impression was operationalized as the time elapsed between the moment they first viewed the Web site and the moment they clicked a link on the homepage. The time it took to form a first impression ranged between 8 and 142 seconds, with a mean of 33 seconds. Table 1 lists the average time for forming a first impression of each of the nine Web sites.

The first three pairs of items in the main questionnaire (items 1–6 in Appendix B) addressed the first research question by asking participants to rate and describe their first impression of the Web site, their expectation to find quality content, and the expectation to find interesting content on the Web site. Respondents were interrupted at the moment of the first click from the homepage and asked to answer these six items. The results are described separately for each pair of items.

TABLE 1. Average time for forming a first impression.

Web site	Average time (secs.)
Valero	31
Medco	40
Weyerhaeuser	26
Westcorp	29
Fred's	23
Equifax	28
Virbac	28
North Coast Energy	62
Horizon Organic	33

First Impression—Summary of Main Themes

When describing their first impression of the Web sites, most respondents referred to colors, links and headings, pictures, visual focus, and the homepage's organization. They made both positive and negative comments about these Web site aspects. Most positive comments were about pictures, links and headings, colors, and organization. For example, one participant commented positively about colors, pictures, and the visual focus ("the thing that grabbed my attention most") on Fred's Web site (note that none of the participants' comments were edited for content, spelling, or grammar):

> Very bright, colorful, very busy. I liked the pictures, helped me to orient what the site was about, but it also had lots of words, so I went to click on the thing that grabbed my attention most... . big letters in a bright color.

Another positive comment illustrates the importance of organization, links, and headings:

> I got a good first impression of the website because of the organization that it seemed to have. I also was able to begin to understand what Weyerhaeuser is by the multiple pictures and link headings.

Most negative comments were about ambiguity, the lack of a visual focus, clutter, and too much text on the page. A typical negative comment about the lack of visual focus is exemplified by this participant's response to Westcorp's Web site:

> There was a lot of words and nothing really caught my attention at first. There was no scrolling headline or anything like that which would come to the reader' [*sic*] attention. All that I noticed was the pictures and I havent gotten any good impression on the website yet, and

normally I would have probably have exited out of it as of right now.

The following negative comment illustrates the themes of clutter and ambiguity. Participants disliked not being able to quickly identify a clear description of the corporation's line of business:

> Initially, I thought that the website looked cluttered. It looks professional with the pictures and icons, etc [*sic*], but there are a lot of words in a relatively small space. The only part I had time to really read was the small introduction under the large "Equifax." It was vague and didn't give me a good idea of what the company actually does. Aside from the cluttered appearance and vague description, the website looks good with several different colors and places to go.

Table 2 presents a list of the recurring themes and their respective frequencies in the participants' descriptions of their first impressions.

First Impression—Frequency Counts

Overall, respondents had positive first impressions of the Web sites. Thirty-five out of the 54 respondents had somewhat positive and positive first impressions. Table 3 lists the frequencies of each rating category and summarizes the kinds of comments respondents in each category made about their first impressions of the Web sites.

First Impression—Median Ratings

All Web sites received somewhat positive first impression median ratings. Table 4 presents the median ratings of first impressions for each of the nine Web sites. Equifax received

TABLE 2. First impression themes.

Theme	No. of positive comments	No. of negative comments	Total no. of comments
Colors (vivid, bright, or dull)	16	2	18
Pictures (liked, disliked, noticed the pictures)	17	0	17
Visual focus (the page was eye catching, something stood out)	8	7	15
Organization (the page was organized, easy, straightforward)	13	0	13
Links (were clear, visible, interesting)	11	1	12
Visual appeal (the page looks attractive, inviting)	9	2	11
Layout (comments about layout, page setup)	9	1	10
Professionalism (the page looks professional)	8	0	8
Ambiguity (vague, ambiguous, unclear, confusing elements)	1	7	8
Clutter (the page was cluttered, disorganized)	1	6	7
Headings (headings, words in large type)	6	0	6
Text quantity (lots of words, lots of text)	1	5	6
Exit (wanted to leave the site immediately)	0	2	2

the lowest median rating (5.5). Respondents reported disliking the large quantity of text on this corporation's homepage, the clutter, lack of visual focus, and ambiguity. They did, however, comment positively about the colors and the bold, visible links

TABLE 3. First impression frequency counts.

Rating	Frequency	Themes
negative	0	
somewhat negative	3	(–) visual focus, exit, clutter, ambiguity, text quantity
neutral	16	(+) links and headings, pictures, professionalism, organization, layout, colors (–) visual focus, ambiguity, text quantity, colors
somewhat positive	26	(+) colors, links and headings, organization, pictures, layout, visual focus (–) visual focus, text quantity, clutter, visual appeal
positive	9	(+) pictures, visual appeal, colors, links and headings, organization, professionalism, visual focus, layout

Note. (–) indicates a string of negative comments. (+) indicates a string of positive comments.

TABLE 4. Median first impression ratings.

Web site	Median rating
Valero	8.5
Fred's	8.0
North Coast Energy	7.5
Virbac	7.5
Horizon Organic	7.0
Westcorp	7.0
Weyerhaeuser	7.0
Medco	6.0
Equifax	5.5

and headings. On the other hand, the participants who looked at Valero's Web site (which received the highest median rating) commented about the appealing pictures on the homepage that provided a strong visual focus. The following two comments, the first about Equifax and the second about Virbac, illustrate these themes.

> I did not see anything special about this website. Nothing caught my eye and made me want to stay at the site to learn more about it. It wasn't eye-capturing. It is just a lot of black words mostly.

> I had a very good first impression of the website. The pictures are very vivid and bright. It is very appealing and caught my eye immediately. It looks very professional.

The second pair of items pertaining to the first research question asked participants whether they expected to find quality content on the Web site and to explain what Web site aspects made them feel that way. The answer choices for the quantitative item were just *yes* and *no*, because a high degree of differentiation was not considered necessary. After all, one either does or does not hold an expectation. The same rationale was used in the dichotomous construction of item 5. The majority of respondents (48 out of 54) answered yes, while only 6 participants did not expect to find quality content on the Web site they were exposed to. Thirty of the participants who did expect to find quality content stated that their expectation was based on the Web site's appearance and nineteen mentioned the links on the homepage. The following comments illustrate these themes:

> There are a lot of bright, eye-catching photos on the main page that make the website appear user friendly and invit-

ing to visitors. The website looks very professional and has links that were easily accessible for users to find out about the company and their types of products. Everything is simple and easy to use and shows that the company takes pride in making their website easy to use by anyone who visits it. Because they take pride in these aspects of their website, I assume that the content of the website would be of high quality.

I do believe that I will find good quality content on this page because of the links that I saw. These links were about their products, facts, what it is used for. It also seemed to be clear and easy for me to use which would make me more willing to search for the information.

The comprehensive list of links and the FAQ are usually god [*sic*] indicators of a thorough and valuable website.

The six respondents who did not expect to find quality content on the Web sites provided a variety of reasons, ranging from general mistrust and disinterest in corporate Web sites to the uninviting appearance of the Web sites they were looking at. For example, one participant wrote:

The fact that it does not seem to be very inviting, I am bombarded with a bunch of different things from real estate to timberland but I don;t [*sic*] see any offical [*sic*] introduction as to what this company does.

The third pair of items asked participants whether they expect to find interesting content on the Web sites, and invited them to explain what Web site elements make them think they would or would not. Thirty-six respondents answered yes, 17 answered no, and 1 did not choose either of the two options. Of those who answered yes, 16 mentioned that they had noticed something on the Web site that teased their interest. Other reasons they mentioned was a general interest in the topic, the Web site's professional and inviting appearance, and the fact that since they knew nothing about the corporation whose Web site they were visiting, any information would be interesting. Comments such as the following ones exemplify these themes:

> the first thing i wanted to click on was a link for avoiding identity theft, that is an issue now so i was interested.
>
> The menu bar lists interesting fun topics
>
> Same reason that I expect to find quality content on it. It is very well done and I have very little knowledge on organic products.

The most repeated reasons why respondents did not expect to find interesting content on the Web site was their personal lack of interest in the topic, followed by the Web sites' uninviting appearance:

> It appears that, at first impression, that the website is dealing with energy, which isn't a seemingly interesting topic for me. It definitly [sic] has the potential to provide me with some interesting information, but at first glance I would not think that it would be of any interest to me.
>
> The first screen of the website wasn't even interesting. You would think that the designer would have been sure to make the initial impression (the first screen) interesting if they intended on showing more interesting information on following screens.

In summary, the Web site aspects that most participants attributed their first impressions to were colors, pictures, links, headings, visual focus, layout, organization and other such elements related to the Web site's appearance.

Research Question 2

The second research question asked what Web site elements help Web site visitors maintain their orientation on a Web site. Items 7 and 9 from Appendix C addressed this question (item 8 addressed research question 3). The responses to the second research question are presented here in the same sequence of three reports as used for the first, and other research questions: a summary of main themes, frequency counts, and Web site median ratings.

Research Question 2—Summary of Main Themes

Table 5 presents the main themes respondents referred to when describing the Web site aspects that helped them find their way on each Web site.

As Table 5 shows, participants found aspects related to links and navigation most helpful in helping them stay oriented on the Web site. Although this finding was expected, the comments about specific aspects of navigation respondents found helpful are very interesting. The presence of links and navigation bars

TABLE 5. Research question 2 (orientation) main themes.

Theme	No. of positive comments	No. of negative comments	Total no. of comments
Links and navigation	33	0	33
Site organization	10	1	11
Links grouped in categories	10	0	10
Navigation bar on all pages	9	0	9
Headlines and titles	8	0	8
Interactive features of (drop-down menus, mouse-over effects)	6	0	6
Other tools (site map, search box)	4	0	4
Visibility (bold, short, easy to read)	3	0	3

alone is helpful, but the comments show it is important that the links be arranged in clear categories:

> The website is broken down into major areas such as banking, loans, marketplace, and customer service which allow the audience to first decide the general area they wish to look in. From there it is clear as to what is listed under each area. It was never really confusing as to what I was looking at exactly and where I needed to go if I wanted to look somewhere else.

Another helpful feature of navigation was for the same navigation menu to be consistently present on all pages:

> It was easy to find my way around, because there was the line of links across the top constantly. You could go anywhere at any time without having to go back.

Surprisingly, this group of users also found interactive menus helpful. This is a novel finding. Just a few years ago, usability studies found drop-down navigation menus to be confusing (Nielsen, 2000b), but the participants in this study made positive comments about them:

> The explanatory links at the top of the page, with the extra fall down list made it a lot easier for me to find what I really wanted to look at.

> The menu on the left handside contained drop-down menus that allowed me to remember and recognize where I am and where I have already navigated.

The Web site's organization and the use of bold, visible headlines and titles were other important Web site aspects that participants felt facilitated maintaining orientation. Only few participants used other navigation tools such as site maps and search boxes. The following comment, however, addresses all these three aspects:

> [the] website was strucutred [*sic*] very well. If I was looking for someting specifically it allowed my to look and find by the bold headlines as well as the inde[x] that let you pick a letter find subjects that begain [*sic*] with that specfic [*sic*] letter.

Research Question 2—Frequency Counts

As Table 6 shows, the overwhelming majority of participants had no problems staying oriented on the Web site. Forty-six out of the 54 respondents rated the site's organization as clear or very clear.

The fact that even those who gave the site's organization low ratings made positive comments is explained by the wording of the item, which specifically asked about helpful Web site

TABLE 6. Research question 2 (Web site organization) frequency counts.

Rating	Frequency	Themes
confusing	1	(+) presence of links
somewhat confusing	4	(+) presence of links, other tools
neutral	2	(+) links grouped
somewhat clear	17	(+) presence of links, visible headlines, organization
clear	29	(+) presence of links, navigation bar on all pages, headlines, organization, links grouped in categories
missing data	1	

Note. (–) indicates a string of negative comments. (+) indicates a string of positive comments.

features. The counterpart of this item is discussed with the third research question.

Research Question 2—Median Ratings

Given the overwhelmingly positive ratings presented in Table 6, it comes as no surprise that all nine Web sites' median ratings were very high on item 7. Table 7 lists each Web site's median rating.

In summary, the Web site aspects that helped participants stay oriented on the Web site were mostly related to links and navigation, followed by the sites' overall organization and the use of bold, visible headings. The next research question addresses Web site aspects that participants found confusing and disorienting.

Research Question 3

Because the literature shows that the main Web site aspect that causes confusion and disorientation is navigation, the items corresponding to research question 3 (items 8 and 10 in Appendix C) asked participants to rate the navigation of the Web site on a 10-point *very frustrating–very easy* scale and to list the Web site aspects that they found confusing and disorienting. The

TABLE 7. Research question 2 (Web site organization) median ratings.

Web site	Median rating
Horizon Organic	10.0
Valero	10.0
Fred's	9.0
North Coast Energy	9.0
Weyerhaeuser	8.5
Equifax	8.0
Medco	8.0
Virbac	8.0
Westcorp	8.0

same sequence of three reports in this section summarizes the participants' answers to these items.

Research Question 3—Summary of Main Themes
The most often mentioned theme was that the Web sites were clear, and there were no confusing elements. However, when confusing elements were listed, they mostly had to do with internal inconsistencies or violations of the Web site visitors' expectations, encountered either in the sites' navigation or content, as these comments show:

> I noticed that some of the links had arrows next to them that you were supposed to click on to proceed. I am used to being able to click on the text to proceed to the next page.

> the dead ends i came to when they asked for money, or the ads. Because every link i clicked on that i thought would answer my question of what specificly [*sic*] they do ended in money, it was frustrating

> What i found confusing was how the toolbar on the side did not have the same links as the homepage.

> The picture in the left-hand corner was a key in my initial impression of the company. This picture shows cattle and farmlands with a drill located on them. My impression was that there would be an environmental angle included. I only found information regarding growth potential and bottom line figures.

Visual clutter, problems related to unclear links, difficult or poorly explained information, and ambiguity about the organization's line of business were other Web site aspects participants found confusing. A number of examples that illustrate these themes are given next. Table 8 lists a summary of all the main themes pertaining to research question 3.

TABLE 8. Research question 3 (confusing elements) main themes.

Theme	No. of positive comments	No. of negative comments	Total no. of comments
Nothing was confusing	16	0	16
Inconsistencies, violated expectations	0	10	10
Clutter, too much information	0	9	9
Link problems	0	7	7
Difficult information	0	7	7
Vague company description	0	6	6

I didn't know what was under each title. There was a brief summary of what each title was about along with the picture, but I was not given information as to what other links were on the page after I clicked a title. [link problems]

The content was confusing, but that's just because I'm not a stock broker and was not looking for specific information when I viewed the site. Some of the charts and graphs could use a little more explanation. There seemed to be a lot of data, and not as much interpretation of it for a lay-person. [difficult information]

The identity theft programs that one can purchace [*sic*] were a little confusing in exactly how they work at first. I had to read it over a few times. [difficult information]

Nothing is necessarily confusing except for the fact that I really do not know what Equifax is and there is no explanation for a definition of it really in my sight. [vague company description]

Research Question 3—Frequency Counts

As Table 9 shows, participants rated the Web sites' navigation positively. Only 8 out of the 53 who answered this question found the navigation to be somewhat frustrating or were neutral.

TABLE 9. Research question 3 (navigation) frequency counts.

Rating	Frequency	Themes
frustrating	0	
somewhat frustrating	2	(–) clutter, violated expectations
neutral	6	(–) violated expectations
somewhat easy	9	(–) clutter, violated expectations
easy	36	(+) nothing
		(–) difficult information, violated expectations, link problems, vague organization description, clutter
missing data	1	

Note. (–) indicates a string of negative comments. (+) indicates a string of positive comments.

Research Question 3—Median Ratings

The individual Web sites' median ratings remained high for research question 3, with no major differences among the nine Web sites. Table 10 lists the median ratings.

The answers to the items corresponding to research question 3 show that many participants did not find any Web site elements confusing, and others identified inconsistencies, clutter, link problems, difficult information, and vague company descriptions as confusing and disorienting elements.

Research Question 4

Research question 4 addressed Web site "stickiness," or the ability to conserve visitors by keeping them interested and attempted to find out what Web site elements maintained the participants' interest. No quantitative item asking whether the Web site maintained their interest was attached to this research question because its nature requires a qualitative answer. Visitors stay on or "stick" with the Web site because there are certain elements

TABLE **10.** Research question 3 (navigation) median ratings.

Web site	Median rating
Horizon Organic	10.0
Valero	10.0
Fred's	9.0
North Coast Energy	9.0
Weyerhaeuser	8.5
Equifax	8.0
Medco	8.0
Virbac	8.0
Westcorp	8.0

that maintain their interest. When this interest diffuses, or when the visitors have found the information sought after, they exit the site. So a quantitative item addressing this question would have only two possible answers already manifested in the Web site visitors' staying or leaving behavior. As long as the participants were still browsing the Web site, something did maintain their interest. What is of significance to this research project is what Web site aspects did keep participants interested during their visit.

Item 11 in Appendix C asked participants to list the Web site elements that maintained their interest. The Web site elements that were mentioned most were visual ones, such as pictures, colors, bullets, bold headings, and other layout items. Participants wrote that in the absence of these visual elements they tend to lose interest in a Web site. Table 11 summarizes the main themes and their frequencies and lists examples that illustrate each theme.

In sum, visual elements, a sense of learning something new, relevant topics, special features (such as videos), comparison charts, fun facts, resources, ease of use, and links were the factors that maintained the participants' interest while visiting the Web sites.

TABLE 11. Research question 4 (conservation of visitors) main themes.

Theme	Positive comments	Example
Visual elements	22	The pictures and bright colors made it interesting. If the Web site was just text, it would be boring and not fun to look at.
Learning	14	Learning about the company and what they did held my interst while browsing the Web site. I had never heard of the company before so learning about everything that they did and how big of a company that they were held my interest very well. I was very impressed with the wide range of products that they have.
Relevant/ current topics	10	I really wasn't interested when browsing through this site, but the employment section kept me looking.
Usability (easy to find information, easy to read)	7	the easy reading, it's simple, bold and bright.
Special features	7	I like how you can compare different brands of medications. I find that interesting.
Links and navigation	4	The drop down menu not only allowed me to realize where I am but also showed me other links that may interest me. As I continued to navigate through others, my interest and curiosity was peaked by other links.

Research Question 5

Research question 5 addressed the public relations aspect of the nine Web sites and asked what Web site elements are perceived as relationship building ones. Because organization-public relationships are complex and multidimensional, chapter 3 proposed a series of five research questions, each addressing one organization-public dimension, to answer question 5.

Questions 5a–5e address the dimensions of trust, commitment, involvement, openness, and dialogue. The following five sections, therefore, report the findings for research questions 5a–5e.

Research Question 5a

Research question 5a addressed the organization-public dimension of trust. Items 12 and 13 in Appendix C correspond to this research question. Item 12 asked participants to rate the extent to which they feel they can trust the organization whose Web site they were visiting. Item 13 asked them what Web site elements make them feel that way. The same series of three reports used for most of the previous questions summarizes their responses.

Research Question 5a—Summary of Main Themes

The main Web site aspect that respondents indicated as a reason why they felt they could trust the organization was information about the organization itself and its values. Visual elements and the overall appearance of the Web site were the next major theme, followed by information quantity, the type of organization, and other themes listed in Table 12. Some participants felt that no matter how good the Web site, they could not trust an organization based on online experience alone. They felt that they needed to do more research, gain first-hand experience, or get recommendations from trusted sources before deciding whether to trust a corporation.

The following comments illustrate the major themes from Table 12. This participant mentions information about the organization and its values, and the presence of contact information:

> They have a lot of information about themselves listed such as their ethics, their corporate profile, and ways that you can get into contact with them. They also have a FAQs page.

TABLE 12. Research question 5a (trust) main themes.

Theme	No. of positive comments	No. of negative comments	Total no. of comments
History, background of the organization	12	4	16
Visual elements, appearance	12	2	14
Organizational values	10	1	11
Web site not enough to establish trust	0	10	10
Information quantity	10	0	10
Seems trustworthy, professional (no specific reason)	7	2	9
Type of company (large, old, small)	8	0	8
Warm, friendly tone	5	2	7
Straightforward, open, clear tone	5	1	6
Contact information provided	6	0	6
Metacommunication (this tells me the organization wants me to...)	5	0	5
References to other organizations (NYSE, seals of approval)	3	0	3

Another respondent makes a negative comment about the pictures on Horizon Organic's Web site:

> There are too many jumping cows and fun pictures. True the website should have fun pictures but at the same time I believe they should have a certain amount of professional pictures to gain people trust. Because most people trust something that is very professional.

This response illustrates the importance of the Web site's appearance:

> Friendly pictures of people and their dogs as well as a professionally designed site that made it appear that the company was dedicated to its cause.

For some participants, however, a Web site alone is not enough grounds for deciding whether to trust an organization or not:

> Well I would have to know more about the organization. The appearance of a website can be deceiving. I would have to research the organization more to determine if I could trust them

Although large quantities of text on a page were perceived negatively when forming a first impression, the mere quantity of information was a factor some participants mentioned to justify their trust in the organization:

> The inclusion of a lot of information, even though I didn't understand it all, makes the organization seem legitimate and trustworthy. The presentation of this information in the frame layout with the attached PDF files also makes the organization seem trustworthy, because they take the time to explain where to go to download the reader, and the reader presentations are very professional. The website looks credible, so the organization does too.

For some participants, being able to place the organization in a category, such as large/small organization, successful, or old provided a reason to trust it:

> The white background makes me think "plan" [plain] or "plain-dealing." All the graphics make me think that it is a smaller company, perhaps owned by an individual... I trust small companies more because they are more likely to care about the communities they serve.

The following answer exemplifies the themes of Web site tone (honest), the presence of contact information, and metacommunication.

> The website seems very honest. They are easy to get a hold of, easily accessible and it seems like they really want my business specifically.

Another comment talks about the metacommunication value of link placement:

> The company presents their background information in a way that makes them sound very reputable. The links to background information were near the top and visible when you first enter the website, which shows that the company wants its visitors to read about the company and their products.

This section has described and illustrated the main themes participants referred to when describing the Web site aspects that they looked at when deciding whether to trust the organization. The next section reports the frequency counts of their ratings.

Research Question 5a—Frequency Counts
Respondents rated their trust in the organizations fairly high. Thirty-eight participants out of the 54 subjects felt they could trust the organization. Table 13 presents the ratings and their frequencies, along with the themes mentioned most by each category of respondents.

Research Question 5a—Median Ratings
The median ratings for trust vary from 5.5 to 10. Despite the variance, the ratings remain positive. Table 14 reports each Web site's median rating.

Participants felt they could trust Horizon Organic's Web site most. Their comments referred to the "good cause" the organization works towards—namely producing healthy, organic products, and other organization values such as the ethical treatment of animals and care for employees. The Web site with the lowest trust rating was Equifax, and these participants' comments explain this low rating:

TABLE 13. Research question 5a (trust) frequency counts.

Rating	Frequency	Themes
can't trust at all	0	
can't trust	4	(–) Web site not enough
neutral	11	(–) Web site not enough
		(+) visual elements, type of company, information quantity
trust somewhat	19	(–) Web site not enough, background information
		(+) background information, company values, information quantity, visual elements, tone, contact information, references to other organizations
trust very much	19	(+) company values, background information, visual elements, tone, information quantity, metacommunication, contact information
missing data	1	

Note. (–) indicates a string of negative comments. (+) indicates a string of positive comments.

TABLE 14. Research question 5a (trust) median ratings.

Web site	Median rating
Horizon Organic	10.0
Weyerhaeuser	9.0
Fred's	8.5
Virbac	8.5
Westcorp	8.0
Medco	7.5
North Coast Energy	7.5
Valero	7.5
Equifax	5.5

> As mentioned earlier, their tactics and reasoning come off as "gimmicky." I found myself thinking sarcastically to myself "Oh my gosh! How did I ever survive without Equifax?!"

> i haven't come across anything that says what exactly this company can do to help me. So the trust was not developed. The website continued to tell me i needed help because there were theives that could take my identity and in order to prevent this i needed to pay money.

In summary, respondents referred to a large variety of Web site aspects when discussing trust. However, one aspect that was mentioned more than any other was the information about the organization, its history, products, and business, as well as the values it stands for. This theme appeared mostly in positive comments, but also in some of the negative comments of Web site visitors who either could not find this information, or they were not satisfied with it.

Research Question 5b

Research question 5b addressed the organization-public dimension of commitment. Ledingham and Bruning (1998) define commitment as the decision to maintain a relationship. Items 14 and 15 in Appendix C asked research participants whether they felt the organization whose Web site they were visiting was interested in maintaining a relationship with them and to describe the Web site aspects that make them feel that way. This section presents the answers to these two items.

Research Question 5b—Summary of Main Themes

Table 15 lists the main themes participants addressed when describing the Web site aspects that made them feel the organization was interested in maintaining a relationship with them.

TABLE **15.** Research question 5b (commitment) main themes.

Theme	No. of positive comments	No. of negative comments	Total no. of comments
Consumer orientation (the Web site/ company is consumer oriented, values, cares about customers)	18	5	23
Contact information provided	12	0	12
Business relations only	8	3	11
Pictures (show ordinary people, people like me)	8	1	9
I (do not) identify with their target public	5	2	7
Usability (Web site is easy, accessible)	5	1	6
Metacommunication	5	0	5
Login (can create an account/login for return visits)	4	0	4

The most often mentioned theme was that of consumer orientation. Participants felt that a consumer-oriented Web site is an indication that the organization is interested in maintaining a relationship with them. The following comments illustrate the Web site aspects that respondents associated with the presence or absence of a consumer orientation:

> The website makes the store seem like it really cares about each individual customer. All of the information is easily accessible, which therefore makes the reader/ customer feel that the store and the people who run the store are just as easily accessible.

> They seem to be quite customer oriented. Their investor relations page noted that they could package and formulate the medicines to fit your needs from a "0.5 oz bottle to a 55 gallon drum." The site that offered a store locator indicates that they want your business and they want to make themselves available to you. On what seemed to be every page there was a link to contact the company

which was nice, there was also a graphic of the actual headquarters of the company which was nice to see.

I think that they showed you alot of pictures with people shaking eachothers [*sic*] hands and people smiling with the people from the company to make you think that they do. But I think that the website looks too generic for them to actually care on an individual basis.

Some respondents commented about the nature of the relationship they perceived the organizations were trying to establish. While some of them thought that doing business was enough in terms of relationship maintenance, others felt dissatisfied with the business-only orientation:

Equifax obviously wants people to pay the $9.95 per month for their Gold membership services, so a good relationship with their customers is a top shelf priority.

There was nothing in the website that made me feel that they wanted more than my money at any time.

An important aspect of relationship building that emerged from the participants' answers was the importance of helping Web site visitors identify with the organization's publics. Photographs played an important role in these Web site visitors' perception that the organization was interested (or not) in maintaining a relationship with people like them:

With me personally? No. Once I'm out of college and have a fulltime and steady job. Yes. The website doesn't have any pictures of people my age, they're all (estimating) in at least their mid 20s or older. It's not pertaining too much to students.

When discussing the commitment aspect of their public relations Web site user experience, some participants interpreted

Web site aspects such as usability, appearance, the presence of contact information, and the possibility to create an account as metacommunication about the organizations' relationship-building intentions, as the following examples show.

> The fact that the website is so user friendly definitely shows that the company is interested in maintaining a relationship with its customers and the general public. There are eye-catching pictures to draw people in and a nice list of links that make navigation easy. Had the website been messy or hard to use, I would have felt the company didn't care what their customers thought or that they were trying to hide information about themselves from the public.

> They gave a lot of ways to contact different people if you had questions or maybe needed some kind of help so that made me feel as though they cared about their customers and stock holders.

> When I first saw the website it asked for a log in name, which suggest to me that they wanted to maintain relationships with thier consumers and people who surf there [*sic*] site.

Research Question 5b—Frequency Counts
The ratings of the organization's perceived interest in maintaining a relationship with these Web site visitors are mostly positive, with 32 out of the 53 participants who answered this question providing ratings of 7 and above. Table 16 breaks down the participants' ratings.

Research Question 5b—Median Ratings
Table 17 presents each organization's median ratings. Westcorp received the lowest rating mainly because participants did not

identify with this financial institution's target public. Horizon
Organic received the highest rating. Respondents liked this Web

TABLE 16. Research question 5b (commitment) frequency counts.

Rating	Frequency	Themes
not at all interested (in maintaining a relationship with me)	2	(−) did not identify with the target public
rather not interested	5	(−) consumer orientation
neutral	14	(+) business relationship only, contact information provided (−) did not identify with the target public
somewhat interested	15	(+) consumer orientation, pictures, contact information provided, Web site usability
very much interested	17	(+) consumer orientation, contact information provided, metacommunication, business relationship only, pictures, Web site usability
missing data	1	

Note. (−) indicates a string of negative comments. (+) indicates a string of positive comments.

TABLE 17. Research question 5b (commitment) median ratings.

Web site	Median rating
Horizon Organic	9.0
Valero	8.5
Weyerhaeuser	8.5
Fred's	8.0
Medco	7.5
Virbac	6.5
Equifax	6.0
North Coast Energy	6.0
Westcorp	5.5

site's consumer orientation and overall appeal, as illustrated by the following comment:

> They give information where you can contact them. They also give in-depth information about every product so you will recognize them and purchase them. They also include games for children. This site seems geared for the whole family and catered so that the consumer will want to revisit it.

In short, Web site aspects such as overall appearance and usability, the presence of contact information, photographs, and content elements were identified by research participants as indicators of the organization's consumer orientation and commitment to maintaining a relationship with publics. Commitment was the second organization-public relationship dimension. The third one, involvement, was addressed by research question 5c.

Research Question 5c

Ledingham and Bruning (1998) defined involvement, or investment, as the time, energy, and other resources an organization is willing to devote to build a relationship. Social responsibility and community involvement, or building communal relationships, are considered indicators of organizational involvement (Bruning & Ledingham, 1998, 1999, 2000; Hon & J. E. Grunig, 1999; Ledingham, 2000; Ledingham & Bruning, 1998, 2000). Hon and J. E. Grunig operationalized this dimension with items referring to the organization's helping behavior. A similar item, item 16 in Appendix C, was used to address research question 8. Item 16 presented respondents with the question: Do you feel this organization enjoys helping others? Item 17 asked them what Web site aspects make them feel that way. The next section reports the main themes participants addressed in their answers.

Research Question 5c—Summary of Main Themes

When answering question 17, most respondents mentioned the organizations' values, community involvement, and stances on issues, which they found in mission and issue statements. Another often mentioned theme was that the organization helps others through the very nature of its business. This theme was mentioned especially in relation to Horizon Organic's and Virbac's Web sites. The pictures, the Web site's usability and overall appearance, and the presence of resources not directly related to the organization's bottom line were other Web site aspects participants mentioned. Some participants, however, felt that the organizations' ultimate profit motive offsets any charity efforts. Table 18 presents a summary of these main themes.

To illustrate these themes, the remainder of this section provides a series of examples. The themes are listed in brackets after each example.

> In the description of the company, they mention the types of gasolines that they produce and how they are conserving resources, which definitely helps others and shows

TABLE **18.** Research question 5c (involvement) main themes.

Theme	No. of positive comments	No. of negative comments	Total no. of comments
Issues and values	11	3	14
Nature of business	13	0	13
Pictures	9	0	9
Profit motive	2	7	9
Web site usability and appearance	7	1	8
No evidence of helping others	0	6	6
Resources	5	0	5
Customer service	4	0	4
They say they (want to) help others	2	1	3

that they are concerned with their customers' opinions and conserving the world's resources, which affects everyone. [Issues and values]

They had a link on the community and what they did for the community in their area. They talked about giving to such organizations like the United Way. [Issues and values]

The pharmacy portion of the site conveys this. It states, "Our wonderful tema [sic] of pharmacists are interested most in the quality of life for their patients." This says to me that Fred's is dedicated to helping others and the smiling pharmacist suggests they enjoy providing help and care. [Nature of business, Customer service]

Like in the previous question the texts are very people oriented, the people look friendly, the colors used are warm colors gives a friendly appeal [Pictures, Web site appearance]

I did not feel that they wanted more than my money. I did not feel that they were going to go out of their way to help any one customer. [Profit motive, No evidence of helping others]

Im [sic] not sure. Perhaps just because they provide information on health conditions to the public that do not appear to benefit their organization. [Resources]

All of their statements say that is what their company is all about. [They say they want to help others]

The next section presents the frequency counts for the items corresponding to this research question.

Research Question 5c—Frequency Counts

Table 19 reports the participants' ratings of their perceptions regarding the organization-public relationship dimension of involvement.

TABLE 19. Research question 5c (involvement) frequency counts.

Rating	Frequency	Themes
does not enjoy helping at all	2	(–) profit motive, no evidence of helping
does not enjoy helping	1	(–) no evidence
neutral	12	(–) no evidence of helping, profit motive (+) nature of business, pictures
enjoys somewhat	21	(–) profit motive (+) Web site usability and appearance, issues and values, nature of business, pictures, resources, customer service
enjoys helping very much	17	(+) issues and values, nature of business, pictures, resources, customer service, Web site usability and appearance
missing data	1	

Note. (–) indicates a string of negative comments. (+) indicates a string of positive comments.

Research Question 5c—Median Ratings

As Table 20 shows, the median ratings were high for all but one Web site. The participants who gave North Coast Energy low ratings commented that the organization's Web site is focused on profit and business, and does not contain any readily available information about its charitable activities.

In sum, the participants' answers indicate that content elements explaining the organization's stance on issues and its values, and communicating how the very nature of its business helps society, were the most important factors in their perceptions of the organization's helping behavior. The Web site's usability and appearance, as well as the pictures, were also important. However, the perception of the profit motive being the major and sometimes

TABLE 20. Research question 5c (involvement) median ratings.

Web site	Median rating
Weyerhaeuser	9.0
Fred's	8.0
Horizon Organic	8.0
Medco	8.0
Valero	8.0
Virbac	8.0
Westcorp	8.0
Equifax	7.0
North Coast Energy	5.0

only focus of the organization was interpreted negatively by participants.

Research Question 5d

Research question 5d addressed the organization-public relationship dimension of openness. Item 18 asked participants to what extent they felt the organization whose Web site they were visiting was open about sharing information, and item 19 asked them to discuss the Web site aspects that made them feel that way. A summary of main themes encountered in participants' answers to item 19 is presented next.

Research Question 5d—Summary of Main Themes

Content elements describing how the organization conducts its business, how the products are made, how the services work, giving information about the organization's history and its executives, and disclosing financial information and policies were mentioned as the major Web site aspects that made respondents think the organizations were open about sharing information. Two other important aspects many participants

TABLE **21.** Research question 5d (openness) main themes.

Theme	No. of positive comments	No. of negative comments	Total no. of comments
Information about the organization	24	3	27
Information quantity	21	1	22
Perceived lack of openness	0	11	11
Contact information available	9	0	9

referred to were the quantity of information available on the Web site and the availability of contact information. Participants who did not think the organizations were open made negative comments about the information being vague, one-sided, or not presented in a straightforward manner. Table 21 lists these themes.

The following comments illustrate the importance of making contact information and extensive amounts of information about the organization available on the Web site:

> They had links to the history of the company and information about their products which made me feel that they were fairly open about sharing information. They also had a list of annual incomes and even the number of employees, so the company is probably open about sharing their information.

> The volume of information makes it seem like they have little to hide and are open about information. Also, the ability to search the SEC Filings for specific content makes it seem like they want the information accessible as well as available.

> Products page features their latest items. They give the contact information for their "corporate headquarters" not just "customer service."

TABLE 22. Research question 5d (openness) frequency counts.

Rating	Frequency	Themes
not open at all	2	(–) not open (not straightforward)
not open	1	
Neutral	12	(–) not open (hiding information) (+) information about the organization, information quantity
somewhat open	15	(–) not open (one-sided) (+) information about the organization, information quantity, contact information
very open	23	(+) information quantity, information about the organization, contact information
missing data	1	

Note. (–) indicates a string of negative comments. (+) indicates a string of positive comments.

Some Web site aspects related to the way the information was presented were perceived as indicators that the organization was not open about sharing information, as these comments show:

> I do not think this organization is very open. It seems like they beat around the bush in most of the information and never really give a fully straight answer on the website. I think this is due to the lack of details on the main page or the feeling that it is hard to find what this company is all about.

> I feel this corporation is very open with its monetary figures and information regarding expansions, but I felt they hid the details of the environmental issues involved in drilling organizations.

> Somewhat, but there seems to be only positive information, therefore, it is difficult to say whether negative information about the company would be presented on this website.

Despite the negative comments, the participants rated the organizations' openness highly. The following section presents these ratings.

Research Question 5d—Frequency Counts
Table 22 presents the participants' ratings of the organizations' openness. Although more than three participants made negative comments, only three actually gave low and very low ratings.

Research Question 5d—Median Ratings
As the frequency counts in the previous section suggest, all the Web sites received high median ratings on the organization-public relationship dimension of openness. Table 23 lists the median ratings.

The participants who gave Horizon Organic very high ratings mentioned the large quantity of information available on the Web site and the effective explanations of organic products.

The quality and quantity of the information presented were the most important factors participants mentioned in their evaluations of the organizations' openness. Although some participants made negative comments that indicated they were suspicious of some organizations' openness, the overall ratings were high or very high for all the Web sites.

Research Question 5e
Research question 5e addressed the fifth dimension of organization-public relationships—dialogue. Two-way communication is a necessary prerequisite of dialogue. Because the Web site itself is one-way communication from the organization to visitors, item 20 asked about the perceived organizations' interest in listening to their publics. Item 21 invited participants to indicate the Web

TABLE **23.** Research question 5d (openness) median ratings.

Web site	Median rating
Horizon Organic	10.0
Fred's	9.0
Weyerhaeuser	9.0
Valero	8.5
Equifax	7.0
Medco	7.0
North Coast Energy	7.0
Virbac	7.0
Westcorp	7.0

site aspects their perception was based upon. Their answers are summarized next.

Research Question 5e—Summary of Main Themes

The availability of contact information was one Web site aspect many participants mentioned. However, for some participants, the presence of contact information alone was not sufficient. They noticed whether this information was easily available and emphasized, and whether the Web site made an effort to extend an invitation to dialogue. The following comments illustrate this theme:

> First inclination would be yes because there is a customer service area and really an organization cannot get by without one, but the fact that it is clearly at the top with the other main topics or areas of interest says something.

> Yes, because they say so on their page, and also they offer contact information and encourage you to use it.

> somewhat, because it offers contact informaton that allows people to provide thier feedback, though it is not a topic that is stressed throughout this website.

Some respondents, such as the one whose comment is cited next, assumed that the organizations would be interested in listening:

> If they weren't interested in listening to people like us, they wouldn't be one of the top successful countries [companies] in the world. Their business relies on support from their customers and if customers are unhappy, their profits will decrease.

Six participants' responses indicate they were not at all impressed with the organizations' interest in listening. Two of their comments are cited as follows.

> It seems to me that they are not talking about what they do for a reason. And whatever the reason is I am sure they wont [sic] care how I felt about it. They simple [sic] want me to buy it.

> Nothing in the website made me beleive they would listen to me more than any other company.

A few participants felt that the organizations were interested in listening, but not to them because they did not identify with the target audiences.

> I doubt that they're interested in what I have to say because I'm not a potential customer of theirs for the next few years. I don't know how far in the future they're looking, so they might want to hear from college freshman, but who knows?

Other participants pointed out evidence on the Web sites that the organizations had listened to their publics in the past.

> There was area for contact and it posted articles about delays in projects because people were concerned about wildlife and such.

Table 24 presents a summary of the main themes for item 21.

TABLE 24. Research question 5e (dialogue) main themes.

Theme	No. of positive comments	No. of negative comments	Total no. of comments
Presence/Absence of contact information	16	7	23
Contact information emphasized	7	4	11
Assuming the organization is/is not interested in listening	6	0	6
Not interested in listening	0	6	6
Not interested in listening to me	0	4	4
Evidence of having listened	3	0	3

Research Question 5e—Frequency Counts

Table 25 presents the responses to the organizations' interest in listening. Fifteen participants rated this interest as neutral, and almost half gave it positive ratings.

Research Question 5e—Median Ratings

The median ratings for dialogue, as Table 26 shows, are less homogenous than those for previous dimensions. North Coast Energy received the lowest median rating. The two participants who gave it the lowest ratings indicated that they did not identify with the organization's target public, and that they were disappointed by the mere presence of a contact link, which was not in any way emphasized. Virbac received the highest median rating. Respondents were impressed with the ubiquitous presence of contact information and the availability of an emergency telephone number.

To summarize, the most important Web site element participants referred to was contact information. The availability of contact information, however, was not always sufficient. Some respondents expected and rewarded attempts to emphasize the

TABLE 25. Research question 5e (dialogue) frequency counts.

Rating	Frequency	Themes
not at all interested in listening	4	(–) not interested in listening to me, absence of contact information
not interested	4	(–) absence of contact information
neutral	15	(–) absence of contact information, contact information not emphasized, not interested in listening, not interested in listening to me (+) presence of contact information
somewhat interested	15	(+) presence of contact information, contact information is emphasized, assuming
very much interested	13	(+) presence of contact information, contact information is emphasized, evidence of having listened, assuming (–) absence of contact information, contact information not emphasized
missing data	3	

Note. (–) indicates a string of negative comments. (+) indicates a string of positive comments.

TABLE 26. Research question 5e (dialogue) median ratings.

Web site	Median rating
Virbac	9.0
Valero	7.5
Weyerhaeuser	7.5
Fred's	7.0
Westcorp	7.0
Medco	6.5
Horizon Organic	6.0
Equifax	5.5
North Coast Energy	5.0

contact information through placement, repetition, or wording, and thus extend an invitation to dialogue.

Research question 5e was the last in the series of five that addressed the public relations dimensions of the Web site user experience. Organization-public relationship aspects were placed in the second phase of the Web site user experience—exploration. The remaining two research questions correspond to the third phase of the Web site user experience—exit.

Research Question 6

As shown in chapter 3, at the moment of exiting a Web site, visitors have formed an opinion of it and have made a decision about the likelihood of return visits. Research question 6 asked about the participants' overall opinion of the Web site. Item 22 invited respondents to rate their opinion of the Web site, and item 23 invited them to describe it. The next section summarizes the main Web site attributes participants referred to when describing their overall opinions.

Research Question 6—Summary of Main Themes

The main Web site characteristics participants mentioned most when describing their overall opinions were appearance, ease of use, and information value, followed by pictures and tone. Table 27 summarizes these themes.

The comments cited next are good examples of one or more of the main themes. The themes are mentioned in parentheses after each comment.

> I'm a big fan of the website, it was fairly inviting, most namely because of hte [*sic*] pictures that were shown throughout the site's pages. It was easy to navigate and quite interesting, with the varying colors and accessable [*sic*] links on the left hand sides of the pages. The text on the site was geared towards a lay person, someone who does

TABLE **27.** Research question 6 (overall evaluation) main themes.

Theme	No. of positive comments	No. of negative comments	Total no. of comments
Web site appearance (organized, professional, appealing, busy, cluttered)	30	10	40
Ease of use (good navigation, information was easy/ hard to find)	27	2	29
Pictures	11	8	19
Tone (clear, straightforward, inviting, friendly, or fake, dishonest)	6	2	8
Informative/Interesting	22	17	5

not necissarilly [*sic*] speak "medical jargon," but is seeking information or bacground [*sic*] on the company or products. [Appearance, Ease of use, Informative, Tone, Pictures]

Everything was easy to find, the information was very useful and interesting. The layout was really neat and professional looking. The pictures were GREAT. [Appearance, Ease of use, Informative/Interesting, Pictures]

Honestly I think it is boring and that has nothing to do with them selling lumber I think that is mainly the layout. [Informative/Interesting, Appearance]

My overall opinion is that it is clear and to the point. The links tell you where you are headed and what information can be found there. With the different pages that outline the different products that are available, there are adequate descriptions as to what that products is [*sic*] for and how it is applied to the pet. The website also allows numerous oppurtunities [*sic*] for pet owners that buy the prodcuts [*sic*] to alert the company of any reactions their pet may have as well as to just submit their comments and suggestions. [Tone, Ease of use]

Overall, the website has a lot of advertising without a lot of quality content. The site map allows easy navigation, making up for the front page confusion. When it really got down to seeing what the company actually does, I was left wanting more. They say all these wonderful things that they'll do for your family or business, but I still have no idea how they do it. [Informative/Interesting, Ease of use]

This section has provided a sense of the respondents' overall opinions of the Web sites. The next one presents their quantitative ratings.

Research Question 6—Frequency Counts
Overall, the ratings indicate that participants formed positive or very positive opinions of the Web sites. Only two reported negative or somewhat negative opinions. Table 28 presents their ratings.

Research Question 6—Median Ratings
Although, as Table 29 shows, the median ratings are overall positive, one organization's relatively low rating stands out. Equifax received the lowest median rating. Overall, the participants who gave it low ratings felt it did not explain its services well or that financial services do not pertain to them. Some wrote about the Web site's uninviting and cluttered appearance.

In short, when describing their overall opinion of the Web site, most comments mentioned appearance and navigation aspects, and some referred to the quality of content, pictures, and tone.

Research Question 7
The last research question addressed return visits. Items 26 and 27 in Appendix C correspond to this research question. The

TABLE 28. Research question 6 (overall evaluation) frequency counts.

Rating	Frequency	Themes
negative	1	(–) appearance, interesting/ informative
somewhat negative	1	(–) interesting/informative
neutral	10	(–) appearance, informative/ interesting, ease of use, tone (+) appearance, informative/ interesting, ease of use
somewhat positive	18	(–) appearance, informative/ interesting, pictures (+) ease of use, informative/ interesting, appearance, pictures
positive	23	(+) appearance, ease of use, informative/interesting, pictures, tone
missing data	1	

Note. (–) indicates a string of negative comments. (+) indicates a string of positive comments.

TABLE 29. Research question 6 (overall evaluation) median ratings.

Web site	Median rating
Fred's	9.0
Horizon Organic	9.0
Weyerhaeuser	9.0
Valero	8.5
Virbac	8.0
Westcorp	8.0
Medco	7.5
North Coast Energy	7.5
Equifax	6.5

quantitative item asked participants how likely they were to visit the same Web site again, and the quantitative one asked them to provide reasons for their decision.

Research Question 7—Summary of Main Themes

One major theme emerged from the respondents' comments. Participants referred to their own needs and interests, and imagined situations that might make it necessary for them to visit the Web site. These comments illustrate the theme:

> I would not visit this website because the topic is not interesting at all to me. It was sort of difficult for me to find what I wanted to read so I would not come back.

> If I was doing a project that required information on animal health care then I would definitely visit this site again. I would not visit it everyday for personal use though.

> I might out of curiosity, or maybe to apply for a job.

> I am currently doing a project on energy in my political science class and I feel that this website might help me in getting more information on energy. I wouldn't come here for solely entertainment, but I could see how I could use this website as a reference for other things in the future.

> Yes, I would dffiniatly [sic] visit this site again. If I need to know any imforamtion [sic] pertaining tomy [sic] health or the health of others I would in fact rearch [sic] this site again for information.

The quantitative answers indicating the likelihood of return visits are presented next.

Research Question 7—Frequency Counts

Less than half of the participants (20) indicated some intention to return to the Web site they examined. Some participants explained that they did not identify with the organization's target public, and others stated they had little or no interest in the organization's products or services. Table 30 presents their ratings.

Research Question 7—Median Ratings

Table 31 presents each Web site's median score. Participants were most likely to return to Valero's, Medco's, and Horizon Organic's Web sites and least likely to revisit Equifax's, Virbac's, and North Coast Energy's Web sites.

The median ratings point out an interesting contradiction: Although both Valero and North Coast Energy are energy companies and their Web sites address similar topics, participants rated their intentions to return to these Web sites very differently. This difference indicates that there might be another reason other than interest in the topic that motivates return visits. A review of the participants' comments about these Web sites

TABLE **30.** Research question 7 (return visits) frequency counts.

Rating	Frequency
definitely no	15
probably no	7
neutral	11
probably yes	17
definitely yes	3
missing data	1

TABLE **31.** Research question 7 (return visits) median ratings.

Web site	Median rating
Horizon Organic	7.0
Medco	7.0
Valero	7.0
Weyerhaeuser	6.0
Westcorp	5.0
Fred's	4.5
Equifax	2.5
North Coast Energy	2.5
Virbac	2.0

does reveal some differences. Although all the 12 participants who visited these two Web sites stated they would return to the Web site if they had a reason or need, those who visited Valero also inserted comments about the quality of the Web site, such as this one:

> It is a very good web page, if you are interested in this company. However, unless I have a reason to visit it again, I don't know why I would ever need to find out more information on it.

On the other hand, one of the participants who visited North Coast Energy's Web site made a negative comment about the Web site's appearance:

> Probably not, it really does not interest me. Nothing really stands out, or catches my attention.

Although these comments do not exhaust the possibilities, they provide some insight into the puzzling difference in the ratings of these two Web sites and suggest that in addition to interest in the topic, the Web site's appearance plays a role in the participants' decision to return.

Question 28 asked participants to provide additional comments. Only 18 participants wrote comments. Overall, these comments did not contribute new insights into their Web site experience. Of the 18 participants who provided other comments, 12 stated that they liked the Web site, 4 offered suggestions for changing certain aspects of the Web site, and two actually wrote that they did not have additional comments.

Question 29 asked whether participants understood the questions they had to answer. Overall, the participants rated the questions as clear and very clear. Only 3 respondents' ratings were lower than 7.

This section has presented the results for the twelve research questions advanced in chapter 3. The results showed what Web site aspects Web site visitors pay attention to at different points of the Web site experience. The following section discusses these results and integrates them into the framework proposed in chapter 3.

DISCUSSION

The main purpose of collecting data to answer the twelve research questions was to connect the temporal and spatial dimensions of the public relations Web site experience. Taken as a whole, the research questions explored connections between phases of the Web site visit (which belong to the temporal dimension) and aspects of the Web site environment (the spatial dimension). The discussion section integrates the results into a map of these participants' public relations Web site experience.

The discussion section is structured according to the temporal phases of the Web site visit: first impression, exploration, and exit. The discussion points out what Web site modules, elements, and element functions (the components of the spatial dimension) play dominant roles during each phase. Conversely, the discussion could be organized according to the structure of the spatial dimension. In this case, the discussion would point out for each Web site module, element, and element function, the moments of the temporal dimension when each spatial component plays an important role. Once again, the temporal dimension is chosen to organize the discussion only because it provides a clear linear structure that is easier to follow than the modular structure of the spatial dimension.

Phase One: First Impression
Data collected in this research study show that the first phase of the public relations Web site experience is very short,

approximately 33 seconds. This finding confirms the observations of Web site usability experts—that users do not take time to examine a site's homepage and form a first impression in a matter of seconds (Nielsen, 2000a; Nielsen & Tahir, 2002). In fact, Nielsen observed that sometimes users abandon a page after only 2–3 seconds (Nielsen, 2000d). The participants in this research study definitely took more than a couple of seconds (but even as little as eight seconds) to examine the homepage. This could be because the instructions they were given to evaluate the Web site or other aspects associated with participating in a research project might have motivated them to examine it more carefully than usual.

The first research question asked what Web site aspects participants noticed in this short period of time and based their first impression on. The recurring themes in their answers indicate that the graphic module dominated this public's formation of a first impression. Most Web site aspects participants referred to were colors, pictures, visual focus, layout, organization, and clutter—all components of the graphic module, as it was defined in chapter 3. In addition to components of the graphic module, participants mentioned large, visible links and headings. The size and visibility of these textual elements, as well as some other comments about the homepage's organization, point out the importance of the organizational function of Web site elements during the first phase of the Web site experience.

In short, the participants' first impression was based on the graphic module and on elements with an organizational function. At an applied level, this finding implies that for this interpretive community, a Web site's appearance is crucial in the formation of a first impression. This finding seemingly contradicts Nielsen's observations that users first look at content and tend not to pay attention to graphics (Nielsen, 2000c, 2000d).

However, Nielsen used a radically different approach and methodology, and studied an older public. Nielsen employed eye tracking to observe what areas of a Web page users look at first. This research posed questions related to Web site visitors' interpretations, and eye tracking would not have helped understand them. In their descriptions of first impressions, this study's participants referred in overwhelming proportions to components of the graphic, not the content module. Although their eyes might have rested on content a fraction of a second before looking at the graphics, it was the graphics they remembered and used to account for the first impressions of the Web site. So, the graphic module played a much more important role in their sense-making than the content module.

The data collected in this study show that the graphic module and Web site elements with an organizational function are the components of the spatial dimension corresponding to the first phase of the temporal dimension.

Phase Two: Exploration
Chapter 3 proposed two steps to the second phase of the Web site experience: orientation and engagement. Research questions 2 and 3 addressed the orientation step, and research questions 4–10 addressed the engagement step. The results corresponding to the orientation step are discussed first.

Step One: Orientation
Gaining a sense of orientation and maintaining it on a Web site can be a fluctuating process in which some steps forward are followed by steps backward. On the one hand, Web site visitors might find that certain Web site aspects help them keep track of where they are, where they have been, and where they can go next in the Web site virtual space. On the other hand, they might

find other Web site aspects disorienting. Research questions 2 and 3 attempted to identify the helpful and disorienting Web site aspects, respectively.

Web designers and Web site usability experts have considered the navigation scheme the most important Web site aspect that helps visitors gain and maintain a sense of orientation (Brinck et al., 2002; Hammerich & Harrison, 2001; IBM, 2003b; Lynch & Horton, 2002; Nielsen, 2000a; Powell, 2002; Spool, 1999; Van Duyne et al., 2003). This study's findings confirm and further this knowledge. When asked what Web site aspects helped them find their way on the Web site, most participants referred to links and navigation menus, both components of the navigation module. The participants' comments also revealed that within the navigation module, elements with an organizational function are very important during the orientation step. The comments reveal that when links are grouped into categories marked by bold, visible headings, or arranged in drop-down menus, they help Web site visitors understand the Web site's structure, which is the basis of gaining orientation on a Web site.

If the navigation module is crucial in gaining orientation, it should follow that a poorly designed navigation module would be the main cause of disorientation. The findings, however, are more complex than that and show that it is not navigation alone that accounts for problems with orientation. Although many respondents did not report any outright disorienting factors, inconsistencies encountered in various aspects of the Web site virtual space as well as violated expectations were perceived as hindrances.

Some inconsistencies pertained to the navigation module, such as differences between the navigation menus on pages of the same Web site. Participants expected the navigation menu to remain the same. Also, if the implementation of the command function was not consistent with their expectations, participants reported problems. For example, one respondent encountered verbal elements that were identified as links (they were underlined) but did not actually have command functionality (a small arrow by their side did). Besides the command function, elements of the navigation module also have a symbolic function. Links are not only used to trigger an action (command function), but also mean something (symbolic function). Some participants reported unclear or misleading link text as a source of disorientation. So, both the symbolic and command functions of navigation elements are very important. Elements with an organizational function were also shown to play an important role. The clutter that resulted from crowding too many elements without organizing them well was another aspect respondents mentioned.

Other inconsistencies were not related to the navigation module. The data show that the content module can also be a source of orientation problems. When components of the content module created expectations that were not met, some Web site visitors became disoriented. This could be because expectations about what content will be encountered on the Web site might influence the structure of the mental map users create. The resulting inconsistencies between the user's mental map and the actual structure of the Web site space can be disorienting. This situation was encountered by research participants when they came across advertisements instead of company descriptions, or when the homepage created expectations that environmental issues would be addressed on the Web site, but were not.

Some research participants reported confusing elements that were not necessarily disorienting, such as information that was too difficult or not well explained. This indicates that the use of the word *confusing* in item 10 was not entirely appropriate, since it was interpreted by some respondents as having to do with comprehension rather than orientation.

Orientation is one of the most important concerns of Web site usability research and has been addressed by many studies. These studies have identified a large number of mistakes and best practices, and have left little room for new findings. Links that do not work as expected, poor link descriptions, and internal inconsistencies have been shown to create problems with Web site orientation (Morville, 1996; Nielsen, 1999a, 2000a, 2000d; Nielsen & Tahir, 2002; Spool, 1999). This study's findings are consistent with results of Web site usability research. Overall, this is a positive indication that although coming from a different perspective, this research taps into the same phenomenon of the Web site user experience. When the orientation research question was proposed in chapter 3, it was also mentioned that it would be interesting to see if this study's findings are consistent with usability research. The fact that they are confirms that this study integrates usability findings into a communication-based framework of the public relations Web site experience, thus contributing to the building of a much-needed bridge between these two areas of inquiry.

Step Two: Engagement

Engagement was proposed in chapter 3 as the second step of the exploration phase. Web site designers as well as public relations scholars recommend creating "sticky" Web sites that maintain users' interest and keep them engaged (Hammerich & Harrison, 2001; Kent & Taylor, 1998; Kyrnin, 2004; Nielsen, 2000a; Powell, 2002). Research question 4 asked what Web site aspects maintained participants' interest in the Web sites they examined. Their answers reveal that engagement is complex and that the content, graphic, and even navigation modules contributed to maintaining interest. It is surprising that respondents made almost as many references to components of the graphic module as to content, which points out that user expectations and perceptions are different for Web sites than for print. Had the participants been asked what kept their interest in a book, they would have most probably referred to content. On the Web, however, content alone does not seem to be king. The data indicate that the graphic and navigation modules play important roles in facilitating access to content and making the Web site experience not only interesting, but also engaging and entertaining.

During the engagement step, Web site visitors have a chance to notice an organization's attempts to engage in relationship building and/or maintenance. Research questions 5a–5e intended to identify the public relations aspects of the Web site user experience and asked participants what Web site elements they associate with various dimensions of the organization-public relationship. The data show that different Web site modules play dominant roles in participants' perceptions of relationship dimensions. As opposed to the first impression phase and orientation step, when the graphic and navigation modules are more predominant, during the engagement step, it is the content module that gains importance. While the graphic content is still present in participants' comments, it is not mentioned quite as often as the content one. For example, when discussing four out of the five relationship dimensions—trust, commitment, involvement, and openness—respondents made more references to components of the content module than to any other module. The graphic module was secondary in their interpretations of all but the openness dimension, where the dialogic module was mentioned after the content one. For the dialogue dimension, the dialogic module was the most often mentioned one, but elements with symbolic and metacommunication functions were also important because participants saw in them efforts on the organization's part to invite them to dialogue.

The finding about the importance of elements with symbolic and metacommunication functions within the dialogic module is a reminder that Web site users' expectations are constantly changing and becoming more and more demanding. The mere presence of contact information, without any additional emphasis or invitation to communicate, was actually perceived negatively by some participants. As early as 1999, Nielsen noticed that users' expectations of Web site usability increase with time and users do not tolerate badly designed Web sites (Nielsen, 1999b). This might be the reason why no blatantly bad Web sites were chosen for this study: Because these kinds of Web sites either do not exist or cannot survive long in the online business world. The nine Web sites belonged to different size corporations, but to successful ones. All Web sites displayed careful and professional design. This is why the high ratings the Web sites received on the quantitative items are not surprising.

So far, this section has discussed the connections between the first two temporal phases and the spatial dimension of the public relations Web site experience. The last phase that remains to be discussed is the exit.

Phase Three: Exit
Research questions 6 and 7 addressed the participants' overall assessments of the Web sites and their intentions to return. These two interpretations are characteristics of the exit phase of the Web site user experience. The data show that the graphic, navigation, and content module were all important parts of the visitors' overall evaluations of the Web site, but the content module plays a leading part in the likelihood of return visits. The dialogic module was not mentioned at all at this stage of the Web site

experience. This could be because users have not yet learned to expect too much out of the dialogic module since corporate Web sites fail to take full advantage of it (Esrock & Leichty, 1998; Gustavsen & Tilley, 2003; Kent et al., 2003; Taylor & Kent, 2004; Taylor et al., 2001). In fact, only one respondent mentioned dialogic components other than contact links and telephone numbers, which also indicates that most users do not yet expect to see discussion forums and chat rooms on corporate Web sites.

Overall, the results showed what roles various elements of the Web site virtual space played in the participants' public relations Web site experience. The results show that elements of the content, graphic, and dialogic module played predominant roles in the participants' interpretations of the five organization-public relationship dimensions. The metacommunication function of graphic and content elements emerged as an important aspect of the public relations Web site experience. Participants interpreted various Web site elements as statements about the organizations' intentions and interest in creating and maintaining relationships with Web site visitors.

CHAPTER SUMMARY

This section has discussed the connections between the temporal and spatial dimensions of the public relations Web site experience that emerged from the data collected. Table 32 summarizes the discussion by mapping out the connections between the temporal and the spatial dimensions of the public relations Web site experience. The first column lists the phases of the temporal dimension. The second column contains the Web site modules that occurred most frequently in the participants' comments about each phase. These modules were inferred based on the top two major themes, as they appear in the summary of

TABLE 32. Connections between the temporal and spatial dimensions.

Temporal dimension	Spatial dimension	
	Modules	Element functions
Phase One: First Impression	Graphic	Organizational*
Phase Two: Exploration		
Step One: Orientation	Navigation	Organizational*
	Graphic	Symbolic*
		Command*
Step Two: Engagement	Content	Symbolic
	Graphic	
Trust	Content	Metacommunication*
	Graphic	
Commitment	Content	Metacommunication*
	Dialogic	
Involvement	Content	Symbolic*
	Graphic	
Openness	Content	Symbolic
	Dialogic	
Dialogue	Dialogic	Symbolic*
	Graphic	Metacommunication*
Phase Three: Exit		
Overall evaluation	Graphic	Organizational
	Navigation	Command
	Content	Symbolic
Return visits	Content	Symbolic

main themes tables (Tables 2, 5, 8, 11, 12, 15, 18, 21, 24, and 27). In phase one, most major themes pointed to components of a single module, the graphic one. In phase three, the comments about the overall evaluation of the Web sites revealed the importance of three modules. In certain instances, as was pointed out in the previous discussion, in addition to Web site modules, certain element functions played an especially important role in participants' comments. In these cases, the elements' functions are marked by an asterisk.

The summary presented in Table 32 answers the two guiding questions of this research study proposed in chapter 3 by pointing out the components of the spatial dimension that played important roles during different phases of the temporal dimension, including the creation of organization-public relationships.

This study has shown how Web site experience analysis can connect the temporal and spatial dimensions of the public relations Web site experience. The mapping of the two dimensions onto each other is likely to differ depending on the interpretive community involved. Further research with different interpretive communities might suggest different links between the temporal and the spatial dimensions which will produce a different map of the public relations Web site experience. This research has demonstrated how the framework can be used to analyze a public's Web site experience. The framework is flexible and can be adapted to different publics and contexts. Possible uses of the framework are discussed in more detail in the next chapter.

CHAPTER 6

CONCLUSION

This research study set out to inquire into the nature and characteristics of the public relations Web site experience. It started from the premises that Web sites are an important communication medium in today's society and that theory is needed to better understand the experience of using them. The study addressed the Web site user experience in the context of public relations. By doing so, it attempted to build a bridge between Web site usability and public relations, and to integrate their findings into a theoretical framework that would address gaps in these two areas of literature. Chapter 3 proposed a framework of the public relations Web site experience built on the major coordinates of time and space. The framework provides a description of three phases of the temporal dimension (first impression, exploration, and exit) and of the components of the spatial dimension (modules, elements, and element functions). A modular view of the structure of the Web site virtual space was proposed. Chapter 3 advanced twelve research questions exploring the connections between the temporal and the spatial dimensions. Empirical research was conducted following a new research protocol called Web site experience analysis. The data analysis, presented in chapter 5, showed how the temporal and spatial dimensions were connected in one public's experience of corporate Web sites and the discussion section mapped out the public relations Web site experience of the student community who participated in this research. The present chapter concludes this study with discussions of this project's contributions to theory and practice, its limitations, and possible directions for future research.

CONTRIBUTIONS TO THEORY AND PRACTICE

This research has generated two products that contribute to theory and practice in the areas of public relations and Web site use studies. The two products are the framework of the public relations Web site experience and the related methodology, Web site experience analysis. For the framework to make a valuable contribution, it first has to meet the criteria for theory outlined in chapter 1. The first part of this section demonstrates that this project has met its goals and discusses the framework of the public relations Web site experience in light of criteria for theory building. The second part of this section proposes a series of uses and applications of the framework and the ensuing methodology and discusses their value for different audiences.

Project Goals

This study's main goal was to create a framework that would explain the public relations Web site experience and understand online organization-public relationship building by answering the question: What aspects of the Web site experience communicate the organization's intentions to build and maintain relationships? The framework proposed here explains that during different phases of the Web site visit, users tend to pay more attention to different aspects of the Web site virtual space. The data collected for this project showed the specific Web site aspects a community of students associated with the relationship dimensions of trust, commitment, involvement, openness, and dialogue. The interpretive, experience-centered perspective that underlies this framework explains that the Web site user experience will be different for different publics. The coordinates of time and space (and their corresponding components) remain constant, but what varies is how the temporal and the spatial dimensions interconnect. For example, a different interpretive community will still experience the first impression, exploration, and exit phases, but might not focus on the graphic module when forming a first impression. Based on the data collected for this research project and on the underlying theoretical assumptions, it cannot be generalized that the temporal and the spatial dimensions will connect in the same manner for different publics. The value of the framework, however, is that its flexibility allows researchers to map out various interpretive communities' Web site experiences with the help of the Web site experience analysis research protocol. To be valuable, a theory should meet the criteria of power, heuristic potential, and importance described in chapter 1. The following sections show how the proposed framework of the public relations Web site experience meets these criteria.

Power Criterion
Power refers to the level at which a theory can operate: description, explanation, and prediction/control (Botan & Hazleton,

1989; Neuman, 1991; Reinard, 1994; Smith, 1988). The proposed framework provides a description of the public relations Web site experience and explains that the nature of each phase along the temporal dimension depends on visitors' interpretations of aspects of the Web site virtual space, thus operating at the description and explanation levels. The prediction and control level depends on a theory's generalizability. Because time and space are fundamental human dimensions, the framework can be applied to different interpretive communities. However, prediction and control are possible only within the boundaries of one interpretive community. For example, based on the map of the Web site user experience that was obtained from data collected from this student community, it can be predicted that other members of the same community will find it relatively difficult to trust Equifax's Web site. Table 14 shows that Equifax received the lowest median rating on the dimension of trust. Based on the knowledge of what aspects of the Web site virtual space this community looks at when deciding to trust an organization, the Web site can be changed so that it communicates more trustworthiness. For example, the research suggests relatively simple solutions that Equifax could implement to increase Web site users' perceptions of trust. One important change would be to explain the company's line of business and the benefits it offers consumers clearly, in detail, without marketing hype. Participants were turned off by vague, ambiguous promises and by the repeated emphasis on the $9.95 monthly fee. They perceived this emphasis as "gimmicky" and interpreted it as "all the organization wants is this money." Instead of emphasizing the price, Equifax should explain and emphasize the benefits it offers. Also, Equifax should have educated the public on identity theft, which at the time of data collection was not well understood. This research also suggests that organizing the Web site better, reducing clutter, using professional photographs of people members of the public can identify with, and making an effort to invite Web site users to interact with the organization are other ways of improving the public relations Web site experience on Equifax's site.

This example shows how the framework can be used at the control level, but only within the confines of the interpretive community whose Web site experience has already been mapped by Web site experience analysis. Further research using the framework of the public relations Web site experience proposed here will be able to refine and test its applicability and thus increase the possibility to use it for prediction and control purposes. This argument also hints to the framework's heuristic potential, or the ability to generate further research. Because a later section of this chapter addresses heuristic potential by pointing out directions for future research, the discussion moves directly to the third criterion of theory development—importance.

Importance Criterion
The proposed framework of the public relations Web site experience is important because it addresses a major gap in the literature about corporate Web sites. This body of literature is characterized by atheoretical lists of recommendations which are not always based on evidence (Durham, 2000). As the literature review showed, not even a systematic definition of user experience could be found in the literature. The proposed framework is a much needed step towards theory development and more systematic approaches to Web site communication. The framework builds upon Web site design recommendations and Web site usability findings and provides a parsimonious structure for integrating them. The framework's importance is also justified by its possible uses and applications, which are discussed next.

Uses and Applications

Chapter 1 discussed the projected utility of a framework of the public relations experience for communication scholars, public relations practitioners, and the general public. This section shows how the framework proposed here and the associated methodology can be useful to each of these three categories of publics.

Communication Scholars

The framework proposed here provides an understanding of the Web site user experience that can help communication scholars produce more informed and more systematic analyses of Web sites. Understanding Web sites and the Web site experience is a necessary prerequisite to studying Web site communication. This study makes the Web site user experience accessible to communication scholars and brings important aspects of online user behavior study into the realm of communication.

In addition to providing a more complete understanding of the Web site user experience, the framework proposed here can be used in communication studies as a lens for analyzing various kinds of communication experiences. The framework itself is modular and flexible. The set of public relations questions used in the engagement step can be replaced with other relevant ones to conduct analyses of different types of Web sites such as health, crisis, risk, and so on. For example, a researcher interested in the online communication of risk can use this framework to research the risk communication Web site user experience of the relevant public(s) and understand what aspects of the Web site virtual space are associated with each public's interpretations of the risk's probability and magnitude, and what Web site aspects might cause public outrage (Sandman, 1993).

Therefore, the value of this framework for the communication scholarly community is that it provides a systematic and integrative lens, or perspective, for looking at Web sites. This lens makes systematic and complete Web site analyses more accessible to scholars without training in technical or design aspects of online communication because it structures the complex phenomenon of Web site experience.

For communication scholars, the public relations Web site experience framework is a new way of looking at Web sites. For public relations practitioners, it can be a tool useful in the creation and enhancement of Web sites. This study's utility to public relations practitioners is discussed next.

Public Relations Practitioners

Public relations practitioners can use this framework of the public relations Web site experience and the Web site experience analysis research protocol to understand, improve, and customize Web site experiences. User experience analysis can be used as a tool for formative research in the development of new public relations Web sites and as an evaluation and improvement tool for already existing ones. So far, Web site research has focused on usability. While it is very important to create usable Web sites, it is also very important to understand the meanings publics create when interacting with these Web sites. Web site experience analysis is not meant to replace Web site usability testing, but to supplement it. Usability is a necessary, but not a sufficient aspect of the public relations Web site experience. This chapter has showed how the data collected with Web site experience analysis can be used as the basis of specific recommendations for improving the public relations Web site experience on Equifax's Web site. So, corporations and public relations practitioners will find Web site experience analysis to be a valuable tool. Finally, the general public can also benefit from this research.

General Public

The Web site experience is a very common and powerful phenomenon. Research on Internet connectivity and online user behavior reviewed in chapter 2 shows that Web sites are a major source of information, and that people use Web sites to make important, even life-changing decisions, such as choosing potential employers or colleges. Given the frequency and importance of the Web site experience, it is beneficial for the general public to understand as much as possible about this daily phenomenon. The framework proposed here provides a relatively simple way of integrating the numerous aspects of the Web site experience and as such can help the general public understand it.

Furthermore, data that result from applying the framework to different contexts by conducting user experience analysis have an information literacy value and help Web site visitors learn from each other's interpretations. For example, when discussing the organization-public relationship dimension of dialogue, some participants were satisfied with the availability of a "Contact us" link, while others interpreted it as lack of interest in listening to publics. By sharing interpretations, Web site users can negotiate the meaning of the presence (or mere presence) of a contact link and change their expectations of Web sites. Given the evolution of corporate Web sites and the public's increasing expectations (Nielsen, 1999b), it is probable that very soon the presence of a contact link will not be sufficient to communicate an interest in dialogue and will be interpreted negatively. In 1998 a content analysis of a representative sample of Fortune 500 companies found that almost 20% of them did not have a contact link (Esrock & Leichty, 1998). These days, the absence of a contact link on a corporate site is not permissible, and this research shows that it might become a component that is taken for granted in the dialogic module. In order to communicate an interest in listening to publics, organizations will have to move beyond the mere presence of contact information and enhance their Web sites' dialogic module. This study's data suggests that changing as little as the placement of the contact link on the page is interpreted as metacommunication about dialogue.

This section has discussed this study's contributions to theory and practice. It has shown that the framework of the public relations Web site experience meets the criteria for theory outlined in chapter 1 and has proposed possible applications and uses of the study's products. Although the research goals have been met, this study is not without limitations. These are discussed next.

LIMITATIONS

This project's main limitations stem from the adoption of the relationship view of public relations as the underlying perspective and the artificiality of the research setting. By adopting the relationship view of public relations as the underling perspective, the study inherits the limitations of the relationship view, which is relatively new and underdeveloped. The artificiality of the research setting also lead to a series of limitations, discussed next.

First, corporations were chosen that participants knew nothing about. It is quite unlikely, although not unheard of, for people to visit the Web sites of corporations they have heard nothing about. Usually, the Web site experience occurs in a context that in this study was artificially removed. This study created an artificial separation between the public relations *Web site* experience and the public relations experience. Usually, the Web site experience is only a part of the more comprehensive, online and offline experience of dealing with an organization. This means that conclusions cannot be drawn from this study about the overall organization-public relationships between the nine organizations whose Web sites were visited and the student community. For example, based on the Web site experience alone, Equifax did not score very well with the participants. However, offline interaction with the corporation and its products could be so positive that it offsets the negative impressions created by the Web site. This study does not address the relationship between the offline and online public relations experiences or their relative weight.

In a context where Web site visitors are familiar with the organization, the Web site experience may be influenced by previous interactions and opinions of the organization. When using this framework to map a public's Web site experience, previous opinions can be taken into account by measuring the offline perceived organization-public relationship using one of the scales reviewed in chapter 2. In this kind of context, it is also possible to add a third open-ended question to each pair of items that address each research question. The third item could ask what aspects of the participant's previous experience of the organization make them feel a certain way about the organization. This way, the participants' open-ended responses could provide insights into the roles offline and online public relations experiences play in their overall perceptions of the organization.

The fact that this study created a separation between offline and online public relations experiences does not mean that the framework can only be used in similar situations. It means that the framework should be adapted to take into consideration the offline public relations experience, and conclusions drawn based on this study's results should take into consideration the study's context.

A second limitation of this study is that people rarely visit Web sites they have little interest in. As these participants' comments showed, many students did not find these Web sites interesting enough to motivate them to visit them again. Some students pointed out that they might return to the Web sites' employment opportunities sections. This suggests that the research protocol could have been slightly modified to increase their interest and create a more realistic context by asking participants to think about employment possibilities as they browsed the Web sites. The participants' lack of interest and involvement could have affected their motivation to process the information and might have lead them to take the peripheral route to processing information (Petty & Cacioppo, 1981). Petty and Cacioppo's elaboration likelihood model predicts that when people process information peripherally, they tend to rely on unimportant message cues. This might explain the frequent occurrence of pictures in the participants' comments. So, this study's conclusions about the importance of the graphic module should be interpreted keeping in mind that lack of motivation might have affected the graphic module's importance.

Third, the physical setting where the research was conducted was also very different from an everyday Web site browsing situation. Data collection was conducted in a small room, with the researcher present at all times. Although the researcher did not look over the participants' shoulders, the small room created a somewhat unnatural and possibly uncomfortable setting. The alternative would have been to make the questionnaire available online, and to ask participants to complete it at their own convenience. However, this would have made it impossible to interrupt them and ask questions about the first impression phase, or to guarantee that they looked at the Web sites before answering the questions. It is possible that the monitored research setting prompted the participants to examine the Web sites more carefully than usual, and to provide more thoughtful answers than they would have in their usual environment. To a certain extent, it is possible that the pressures of the research setting have offset the effects of lack of interest and motivation previously discussed.

Future research might be able to build on this study to create research protocols that allow researchers access to more natural, contextualized Web site experiences. Field observation methods or diaries could be used to research people's long term relationships with Web sites they often return to, such as Internet portals, news Web sites, or Web sites that provide downloads and other resources. The next section suggests more directions for future research.

DIRECTIONS FOR FUTURE RESEARCH

Future research can build upon the framework of the public relations Web site experience proposed in this study and contribute to the Web site user experience and public relations bodies of knowledge. This section outlines four ideas for possible future research.

The first idea is to apply the public relations Web site experience framework to research other interpretive communities, other types of Web sites, and various combinations of the two. The undergraduate student community is one of many interpretive communities that use corporate Web sites. Journalists, investors, business partners, customers, and activists are examples of other interpretive communities who experience corporate Web sites. Moreover, as was explained in chapter 1, corporate Web sites are not the only public relations Web sites. In fact, it can be argued that most, if not all, Web sites, contain a public relations aspect. The framework can be used to analyze the public relations experience of visiting other types of Web sites, such as those of universities, activist groups, nongovernmental organizations, and so forth. When other countries and other cultures are taken into consideration, the combinations of Web sites and interpretive communities become endless.

A second direction for future research is to address the public relations Web site experience in the larger context of public relations experiences and to assess the role Web sites play in the organization-public relationship. A Web site can motivate a person to enter or leave a relationship with an organization. This is often the case with e-commerce Web sites—but what about other types of organizations? For examples, do Web sites play a role in people's decisions to open or close bank accounts? What roles? For what kinds of people? Under what circumstances? The list of questions goes on.

A third direction for future research would involve not looking outside the framework, as the two aforementioned research possibilities have, but inwards. It would be fascinating to fully understand the public relations Web site experience of an interpretive community by finding out the relative importance of various Web site aspects. In this research project, the modules have been identified based on major themes, and the major themes based on the number of occurrences. The data show that the content and graphic modules are important in participants' perceptions of the organizations' openness. But how important are they? Is the content module twice as important as the graphic one? Experimental research with members of an interpretive community could help answer such questions by varying characteristics of the different Web site modules and observing the effects.

Finally, a fourth direction for future research is the further development of this framework. This framework describes only the temporal and spatial dimensions of the public relations Web site experience. But this experience is complex and multidimensional. Further research might explore other facets of the Web site user experience, such as emotion and cognition, and attempt to integrate them into a multidimensional framework.

This section has suggested four possible directions for future research building on the framework of the public relations Web site experience proposed in this study. Although this short list of four is by no means exhaustive, it does demonstrate that the framework has good heuristic potential.

CHAPTER SUMMARY

This chapter provided a short summary of the research project undertaken in this study. Then, it discussed this study's contributions to theory and practice. The discussion showed that the framework of the public relations Web site experience meets the criteria for theory mentioned in chapter 1. It also pointed out how this study's products, namely the public relations experience framework and the Web site experience analysis research protocol, can be useful to three categories of publics: communication scholars, public relations practitioners, and Web site users in general. The project's limitations stemming from the artificiality of the research setting were then discussed. Following the discussion of limitations, this chapter concluded this research by outlining possible directions for future research and thus demonstrating the framework's heuristic potential.

This research study has proposed a framework of the public relations Web site experience structured on the dimensions of time and space. With the help of the Web site experience analysis research protocol, the framework can be used to produce a map of an interpretive community's public relations Web site experience. The research has demonstrated the framework's application and uses by mapping the corporate public relations Web site experience of a student community. The study concluded by discussing possible uses of the framework by different communities, this project's limitations, and directions for future research.

RESEARCH PARTICIPANT CONSENT FORM PROJECT 04-045

Building and Maintaining Relationships Online:
A Framework for Analyzing the Public Relations
Web Site Experience

Dr. Howard Sypher

Purdue University

Department of Communication

PURPOSE OF RESEARCH

This research is being conducted by a member of the Department of Communication at Purdue University. The focus of this study is to try to understand the experience of visiting Web sites. This type of research provides an in-depth understanding of online communication.

SPECIFIC PROCEDURES TO BE USED

As a research participant, I will first answer a series of questions about my background and experience using computers. When the computer prompts me, I will browse the Web site displayed on the screen and try to form an opinion of it. While I am browsing the Web site, the researcher may interrupt me at times and ask me to turn to the other computer and answer some questions about the Web site.

DURATION OF PARTICIPATION

The duration of participation in this research project is estimated to be about 40 minutes.

BENEFITS TO THE INDIVIDUAL

The benefits of participating in this research are increased understanding of how organizations use Web sites to communicate with their publics.

RISKS TO THE INDIVIDUAL

This research involves no foreseeable risks to participants.

CONFIDENTIALITY

I understand that the researcher will employ all possible methods to keep my responses anonymous. I am not to provide my last name, address, or any personal identifying information on any forms other that this informed consent form. I understand that the researcher is under obligation *not* to associate my name from this form to my responses stored in the computer database.

VOLUNTARY NATURE OF PARTICIPATION

I do not have to participate in this research project. If I agree to participate I can withdraw my participation at any time without penalty.

HUMAN SUBJECT STATEMENT:

If I have any questions about this research project, I can contact Dr. Howard Sypher at 494-8603. If I have concerns about the treatment of research participants, I can contact the Committee on the Use of Human Research Subjects at Purdue University, 610 Purdue Mall, Hovde Hall Room 307, West Lafayette, IN 47907-2040. The phone number for the Committee's secretary is (765) 494-5942. The e-mail address is irb@purdue.edu.

I HAVE HAD THE OPPORTUNITY TO READ THIS CONSENT FORM, ASK QUESTIONS ABOUT THE RESEARCH PROJECT AND AM PREPARED TO PARTICIPATE IN THIS PROJECT.

_____   _____

Participant's Signature   Date

_____

Participant's Name

_____   _____

Researcher's Signature   Date

Appendix B

Background Questionnaire

1. Age: _____

2. Sex:

   a) Male
   b) Female

3. Year in college:

   a) Freshman
   b) Junior
   c) Sophomore
   d) Senior

4. How long have you been using a personal computer?

   _____ Years _____ Months

5. How often do you use a personal computer?

   a) Several times a day
   b) Every day
   c) 2–3 times a week
   d) Once a week
   a) 2–3 times a month

6. How long have you been using the Internet?

   _____ Years _____ Months

7.   How frequently do you use the Internet?

    b) Several times a day
    c) Every day
    d) 2–3 times a week
    e) Once a week
    e) 2–3 times a month

8.   Do you enjoy using computers?

    a) Very much
    b) Somewhat
    c) Neutral
    d) Not really
    e) Not at all

9.   Are you familiar with ORGANIZATION NAME?
    a) Very familiar
    b) I've heard the name, but I don't know much about it
    c) Not familiar at all

If your answer was "very familiar," please tell the researcher now.

Appendix C

Main Questionnaire

1. My first impression of this Web site is:
    (very bad) 1 2 3 4 5 6 7 8 9 10 (very good)

2. Please describe your first impressions of the Web site. In your description, point out those Web site aspects that your first impressions are based upon.

3. Do you expect to find good quality content on this Web site?

    a) Yes

    b) No

4. What aspects of the Web site make you feel the way you do?

5. Do you expect to find interesting content on this Web site?

    a) Yes

    b) No

6. What aspects of the Web site make you feel the way you do?

PLEASE CONTINUE BROWSING THE WEB SITE.
WHEN YOU HAVE FORMED AN OPINION OF IT,
RETURN TO THIS QUESTIONNAIRE.

7. The organization of this Web site is:
   (very confusing) 1 2 3 4 5 6 7 8 9 10 (very clear)

8. Navigating the links on this Web site is:
   (very frustrating) 1 2 3 4 5 6 7 8 9 10 (very easy)

9. Please list the aspects of the Web site that help you find
   your way around:

10. Please list the aspects of the Web site that you find con-
    fusing and/or disorienting:

11. What on this Web site maintained your interest while
    browsing the Web site?

12. Do you feel you can trust this organization?
    (not at all) 1 2 3 4 5 6 7 8 9 10 (very much)

13. What on this Web site makes you feel this way?

14. Do you feel this organization is interested in maintaining
    a relationship with you?
    (not at all) 1 2 3 4 5 6 7 8 9 10 (very much)

15. What on this Web site makes you feel this way?

16. Do you think this organization enjoys helping others?
    (not at all) 1 2 3 4 5 6 7 8 9 10 (very much)

17. What on this Web site makes you feel this way?

18. Do you think this organization is open about sharing
    information?
    (not at all) 1 2 3 4 5 6 7 8 9 10 (very much)

19. What on this Web site makes you feel this way?

20. Do you feel that this organization is interested in listening to what people like you have to say?
(not at all) 1 2 3 4 5 6 7 8 9 10 (very much)

21. What on this Web site makes you feel this way?

22. Overall, how do you evaluate this Web site?
(very bad) 1 2 3 4 5 6 7 8 9 10 (very good)

23. Please describe your overall opinion of the *Web site*. In your description, please point out those Web site aspects that your opinion is based upon.

24. *Overall, how would you rate your opinion of this organization?
(very negative) 1 2 3 4 5 6 7 8 9 10 (very positive)

25. *Please describe your overall opinion of [*organization name*]. In your description, please point out those Web site aspects that your opinion is based upon.

26. Would you visit this Web site again?
(definitely no) 1 2 3 4 5 6 7 8 9 10 (definitely yes)

27. Why, or why not?

28. The questions I had to answer about the Web site were:
(very confusing) 1 2 3 4 5 6 7 8 9 10 (very clear)

Note. Items 24 and 25 were included to collect data for a future, related study.

REFERENCES

Aarseth, E. J. (1997). *Cybertext: Perspectives on ergodic literature*. Baltimore: Johns Hopkins University Press.

Aikat, D. (2000). A new medium for organizational communication: Analyzing Web content characteristics of Fortune 500 companies [Electronic version]. *Electronic Journal of Communication, 10*, online. Retrieved March 12, 2002, from http://www.cios.org/www/ejcmain.htm

Alfonso, G.-H., & de Valbuena Miguel, R. (2006). Trends in online media relations: Web-based corporate press rooms in leading international companies. *Public Relations Review, 32*(2), 267–275.

Bennett, R. (2005). Antecedents and consequences of Website atmosphere in online charity fundraising situations. *Journal of Website Promotion, 1*(1), 131–152.

Benoit, W. L., & Benoit, P. J. (2000). The virtual campaign: Presidential primary Websites in Campaign 2000 [Electronic version]. *American Communication Journal, 3*. Retrieved March 12, 2002, from http://acjournal.org/holdings/vol3/Iss3/rogue4/benoit.html

Berman, S. (1999). Public buildings as public relations: Ideas about the theory and practice of strategic architectural communication. *Public Relations Quarterly, 44*(1), 18–22.

Berners-Lee, T. (2002). *Press FAQ*. Retrieved January 6, 2003, from http://www.w3.org/People/Berners-Lee/Internet

Berry, D. (2000). *The user experience.* Retrieved March 23, 2003, from http://www-106.ibm.com/developerworks/web/library/w-berry/

Blair, C., Jeppeson, M. S., & Pucci Jr., E. (1995). Public memorializing in postmodernity: The Vietnam Veterans Memorial as prototype. In C. R. Burgchardt (Ed.), *Readings in rhetorical criticism* (1st ed., pp. 604–630). State College, PA: Strata Publications.

Bostdorff, D. M. (1987). Making light of James Watt: A Burkean approach to the form and attitude of political cartoons. *Quarterly Journal of Speech, 73*(1), 43–59.

Botan, C. H. (1992). International public relations: Critique and reformulation. *Public Relations Review, 18*(2), 149–159.

Botan, C. H., & Hazleton, V. (1989). The role of theory in public relations. In C. H. Botan & V. Hazleton (Eds.), *Public relations theory* (pp. 3–15). Hillsdale, NJ: Lawrence Erlbaum.

Botan, C. H., & Soto, F. (1998). A semiotic approach to the internal functioning of publics: Implications for strategic communication and public relations. *Public Relations Review, 24*(1), 21–44.

Brinck, T., Gergle, D., & Wood, S. D. (2002). *Usability for the Web: Designing Web sites that work* (1st ed.). San Francisco: Morgan Kaufmann Publishers.

Broom, G. M., Casey, S., & Ritchey, J. (1997). Toward a concept and theory of organization-public relationships. *Journal of Public Relations Research, 9*(2), 83–98.

Broom, G. M., Casey, S., & Ritchey, J. (2000). Concept and theory of organization-public relationships. In J. A. Ledingham & S. D. Bruning (Eds.), *Public relations as relationship management.*

A relational approach to the study and practice of public relations (pp. 3–22). Mahwah, NJ: Lawrence Erlbaum Associates.

Bruning, S. D. (2002). Relationship building as retention strategy: Linking relationship attitudes and satisfaction evaluations to behavioral outcomes. *Public Relations Review, 28*(1), 39–48.

Bruning, S. D., & Ledingham, J. A. (1998). Organization-public relationships and consumer satisfaction: The role of relationships in the satisfaction mix. *Communication Research Reports, 15*(2), 198–208.

Bruning, S. D., & Ledingham, J. A. (1999). Relationships between organizations and publics: Development of a multi-dimensional organization-public relationship scale. *Public Relations Review, 25*(2), 157–170.

Bruning, S. D., & Ledingham, J. A. (2000). Perceptions of relationships and evaluations of satisfaction: An exploration of interaction. *Public Relations Review, 26*(1), 85–95.

Brunn, S. D., & Cottle, C. D. (1997). Small states and cyberboosterism. *Geographical Review, 87*(2), 240–258.

Bush, V. (1945). As we may think. *The Athlantic Monthly, 176*, 101–108.

Cailliau, R. (1995). *A little history of the World Wide Web. W3 Consortium.* Retrieved July 16, 2002, from http://www.w3.org/History.html

Callison, C. (2003). Media relations and the Internet: How Fortune 500 company Web sites assist journalists in news gathering. *Public Relations Review, 29*(1), 29–41.

Capriotti, P. (2007). Risk communication strategies in the chemical industry in Spain: An examination of the Web content of companies on issues related to chemical risk. *Journal of Communication Management, 11*(2), 150–169.

Center, A. H., & Jackson, P. (1995). *Public relations practices: Management case studies and problems* (5th ed.). Englewood Cliffs, NJ: Prentice Hall.

Chaudhri, V., & Wang, J. (2007). Communicating corporate social responsibility on the Internet. *Management Communication Quarterly, 21*(2), 232–247.

Chen, Y.-N. K. (2007). A study of journalists' perception of candidates' Websites and thier relationships with the campaign organization in Taiwan's 2004 presidential election. *Public Relations Review, 33*(1), 103–105.

Cockburn, A., & McKenzie, B. (2001). What do Web users do? An empirical analysis of Web use. *International Journal of Human-Computer Studies, 54*(6), 903–922.

comScore Media Matrix. (2008). *2007 online holiday shopping season surpasses $29 billion in sales, up 19 percent versus year ago.* Retrieved February 1, 2008, from http://www.comscore.com/press/release.asp?press=1990

Coombs, W. T. (1998). The Internet as potential equalizer: New leverage for confronting social irresponsibility. *Public Relations Review, 24*(3), 289–303.

Cox, B. (2002). Online sales keep on growing. Retrieved June 27, 2000, from http://cyberatlas.internet.com/markets/retailing/article/0,1323,6061_1151201,00.html

Curtin, P. A., & Gaither, T. K. (2003). International agenda-building in cyberspace: A study of Middle East government English-language Websites. *Public Relations Review, 30*(1), 25–36.

CyberAtlas. (2001). *Online influencers rely on company Web sites.* Retrieved June 21, 2002, from http://cyberatlas.internet.com/ big_picture/demographics/article/0,,5901_944881,00.html

Cyberspace Policy Research Group. (2001). *Website Attribute Evaluation System.* Retrieved February 3, 2002, from http:// www.cyprg.arizona.edu/index.html

Dewey, J. (1927). *The public and its problems.* Chicago: Swallow Press.

DiNardo, A. M. (2002). The Internet as a crisis management tool: A critique of banking sites during Y2K. *Public Relations Review, 28*(4), 367–378.

Dominick, J. R. (1999). Who do you think you are? Personal home pages and self-presentation on the World Wide Web. *Jornalism and Mass Communication Quarterly, 76*(4), 646–658.

Durham, M. (2000). Organizational Websites: How and how well do they communicate? *Australian Journal of Communication, 27*(3), 1–14.

Edwards, J. L., & Winkler, C. K. (1997). Representative form and the visual Ideograph: The Iwo Jima image in editorial cartoons. *Quarterly Journal of Speech, 83*(3), 289–310.

Equifax. (2004). *Equifax Corporate Website.* Retrieved March 22, 2004, from http://www.equifax.com

Esrock, S. L., & Leichty, G. B. (1998). Social responsibility and corporate Web pages: Self-presentation or agenda setting? *Public Relations Review, 24*(3), 305–319.

Esrock, S. L., & Leichty, G. B. (1999). Corporate World Wide Web pages: Serving the news media and other publics. *Jornalism and Mass Communication Quarterly, 76*(3), 456–467.

Esrock, S. L., & Leichty, G. B. (2000). Organization of corporate Web pages: Publics and functions. *Public Relations Review, 26*(3), 327–344.

Eveland, W. P., & Dunwoody, S. (1998). Uses and navigation patterns of a science World Wide Web site for the public. *Public Understanding of Science, 7*(4), 285–311.

Eveland, W. P., & Dunwoody, S. (2000). Examining information processing on the World Wide Web using think-aloud protocols. *Media Psychology, 2*(3), 219–244.

Faiola, A. (2000). *Typography primer*. Sewickley, PA: Graphic Arts Technical Foundation Publishing.

Fish, S. (1980). *Is there a text in this class?* Cambridge, MA: Harvard University Press.

Fish, S. (2001). Yet once more. In J. Machor, L. & P. Goldstein (Eds.), *Reception study: From literary theory to cultural studies* (pp. 29–38). New York: Routledge.

Fisher Liu, B. (2008). Online disaster preparation: Evaluation of state emergency management Web sites. *Natural Hazards Review, 9*(1), 43–48.

Flanagin, A. J., Farinola, W. J. M., & Metzger, M. J. (2002). The technical code of the Internet/World Wide Web. *Critical Studies in Media Communication, 17*(4), 409–428.

Fogg, B. J. (2003, April 5–10). Prominence-interpretation theory: Explaining how people assess credibility online. In *Proceedings of the Conference on Human Factors in Computing Systems*, Ft. Lauderdale, FL (pp. 722–723). New York: ACM Press.

Fogg, B. J., Kameda, T., Boyd, J., Marshall, J., Sethi, R., Sockol, M., and Trowbridge, T. (2002). *Stanford-Makovsky Web Credibility Study 2002: Investigating what makes Web sites credible today* (Research report). Stanford Persuasive Technology Lab & Makovsky & Company, Stanford University.

Fogg, B. J., Marable, L., Stanford, J., & Tauber, E. R. (2002). *How do people evaluate a Web site's credibility? Results from a large study.* Retrieved March 25, 2003, from http://www. webcredibility.org/

Fogg, B. J., Marshall, J., Kameda, T., Solomon, J., & Rangnekar, A. (2002). *Web credibility research: A method for online experiments and early study results.* Retrieved March 20, 2003, from http://www.webcredibility.org/

Foss, S. K. (1986). Ambiguity as persuasion: The Vietnam veterans' memorial. *Communication Quarterly, 34*(3), 326–340.

Fred's. (2004). *Fred's corporate Web site.* Retrieved March 22, 2004, from http://www.fredsinc.com

Fursich, E., & Robins, M. (2002). Africa.com: The self-representation of sub-Saharan nations on the World Wide Web. *Critical Studies in Media Communication, 19*(2), 190–211.

Fursich, E., & Robins, M. (2004). Visiting Africa: Constructions of nation and identity on travel Websites. *Journal of Asian and African Studies, 39*(1–2), 133–152.

Global Reach. (2004). *Global Internet statistics.* Retrieved July 15, 2004, from http://www.glreach.com/globstats/

Goldie, P. (2003). *Experience matters—More now than ever.* Retrieved March 25, 2003, from http://www.macromedia. com/newsletters/edge/march2003/section0.html

Grunig, J. E. (1993). Image and substance: From symbolic to behavioral relationships. *Public Relations Review, 19*(2), 121–139.

Grunig, J. E. (2002). *Qualitative methods for assessing relationships between organizations and publics* [Electronic version]. Institute for Public Relations. Retrieved September 7, 2002, from http://www.instituteforpr.com

Grunig, J. E., & Huang, Y.-H. (2000). From organizational effectiveness to relationship indicators: Antecedents of relationships, public relations strategies, and relationship outcomes. In J. A. Ledingham & S. D. Bruning (Eds.), *Public relations as relationship management: A relational approach to the study and practice of public relations* (pp. 23–53). Mahwah, NJ: Lawrence Erlbaum Associates.

Grunig, J. E., & Hunt, T. (1984). *Managing public relations.* New York: Holt, Rinehart, and Winston.

Grunig, J. E., & IABC Research Foundation. (1992). *Excellence in public relations and communication management.* Hillsdale, NJ: Lawrence Erlbaum Associates.

Grunig, L. A., Grunig, J. E., & Dozier, D. M. (2002). *Excellent public relations and effective organizations.* Mahwah, NJ: Lawrence Erlbaum Associates.

Gustavsen, P. A., & Tilley, E. (2003). Public relations communication through corporate Websites: Towards an understanding of the role of interactivity [Electronic version]. *PRism, 1.* Retrieved September 3, 2002, from http://www.praxis.bond.edu.au/prism/papers/refereed/paper5.pdf

Hallahan, K. (2003). *A model for assessing Web sites as tools in building organizational-public relationships.* Paper presented at the International Communication Association Convention, San Diego.

Hammerich, I., & Harrison, C. (2001). *Developing online content: The principles of writing and editing for the Web.* New York: John Wiley & Sons.

Hawes, L. C. (1975). *Pragmatics of analoguing: Theory and model construction in communication.* Reading, MA: Addison-Wesley.

Heath, R. L. (1993). A rhetorical approach to zones of meaning and organizational prerogatives. *Public Relations Review, 19*(2), 141–155.

Heath, R. L. (1998). New communication technologies: An issues management point of view. *Public Relations Review, 24*(3), 273–288.

Heath, R. L. (2000). A rhetorical perspective on the values of public relations: Crossroads and pathways toward concurrence. *Journal of Public Relations Research, 12*(1), 69–91.

Hernon, P. (1998). Government on the Web: A comparison between the United States and New Zealand. *Government Information Quarterly, 15*(4), 419–443.

Hobbes, R. (2002). *Hobbes' Internet timeline.* Retrieved July 16, 2002, from http://www.zakon.org/robert/internet/timeline/

Hon, L., & Grunig, J. E. (1999). *Guidelines for measuring relationships in public relations* [Electronic version]. Institute for Public Relations. Retrieved September 2, 2002, from http://www.instituteforpr.com/pdf/1999_guide_measure_relationships.pdf

Horizon Organic. (2004). *Horizon Organic corporate Web site.* Retrieved March 24, 2004, from http://www.horizonorganic.com/

Huang, Y.-H. (2001). OPRA: A cross-cultural, multiple item scale for measuring organization-public relationships. *Journal of Public Relations Research, 13*(1), 61–90.

Huizingh, E. K. R. E. (2000). The content and design of Web sites: An empirical study. *Information and Management, 37*(3), 123–134.

Hurst, M., & Gellady, E. (1999). *Building a great customer experience to develop brand, increase loyalty, and grow revenues* [White paper]. Creative Good. Retrieved March 10, 2003, from http://www.creativegood.com/creativegood-whitepaper.pdf

IBM. (2003a). *IBM ease of use Web site: Business view section.* Retrieved March 20, 2003, from http://www-3.ibm.com/ibm/easy/eou_ext.nsf/Publish/550

IBM. (2003b). *IBM ease of use Web site: Web design guidelines.* Retrieved March 20, 2003, from http://www-3.ibm.com/ibm/easy/eou_ext.nsf/Publish/572

Internet World Stats. (2008). *Internet usage statistics.* Retrieved February 1, 2008, from http://www.internetworldstats.com/stats.htm

Jackson, M. H., & Purcell, D. (1997). Politics and media richness in World Wide Web representations of the former Yugoslavia. *Geographical Review, 87*(2), 233–253.

Jo, S., & Jung, J. (2005). A cross-cultural study of the World Wide Web and public relations. *Corporate Communications: An International Journal, 10*(1), 24–40.

Jo, S., & Kim, Y. (2003). The effect of Web characteristics on relationship building. *Journal of Public Relations Research, 15*(3), 199–233.

Johnson, M. A. (1997). Public relations and technology: Practitioner perspectives. *Journal of Public Relations Research, 9*(3), 213–236.

Johnson, S. (1997). *Interface culture: How new technology transforms the way we create and communicate.* San Francisco: HarperEdge.

Joyce, M. (1990). *Afternoon, a story.* (Hypertext ed.). Cambridge, MA: Eastgate Press.

Jupiter Media Metrix. (2002). *Corporate spending on Web sites remains high, but focused on internal initiatives.* Retrieved March 25, 2003, from http://www.jupiterresearch.com/xp/jmm/press/2002/pr_041002.html

Kang, S., & Norton, H. E. (2004). Nonprofit organizations' use of the World Wide Web: Are they sufficiently fulfilling organizational goals? *Public Relations Review, 30*(3), 279–284.

Kant, I. (1787/2003). *Critique of pure reason* (2nd ed., N. Kemp Smith, Trans.). New York: Palgrave Macmillan.

Kent, M. L., & Taylor, M. (1998). Building dialogic relationships through the World Wide Web. *Public Relations Review, 24*(3), 321–334.

Kent, M. L., & Taylor, M. (2002). Toward a dialogic theory of public relations. *Public Relations Review, 28*(1), 21–37.

Kent, M. L., Taylor, M., & White, W. J. (2003). The relationship between Web site design and organizational responsiveness to stakeholders. *Public Relations Review, 29*(1), 63–77.

Ki, E.-J., & Hon, L. (2006). Relationship maintenance strategies on Fortune 500 company Web sites. *Journal of Communication Management, 10*(1), 27–43.

Kim, S. T., & Weaver, D. (2002). Communication research about the Internet: A thematic meta-analysis. *New Media & Society, 4*(4), 518–538.

Kim, Y. (2001). Searching for the organization-public relationship: A valid and reliable instrument. *Journalism and Mass Communication Quarterly, 78*(4), 799–815.

Klotz, R. (1998). Virtual criticism: Negative advertising on the Internet in the 1996 Senate races. *Political Communication, 15*(3), 347–365.

Koyani, S. J., & Bailey, R. W. (2002). *Searching vs. linking on the Web: A summary of the research*. Rockville, MD: Office of Communications—National Cancer Institute.

Kuchi, T. (2006). Communicating mission: An analysis of academic library Web sites. *The Journal of Academic Librarianship, 32*(2), 148–154.

Kyrnin, J. (2004). *"Sticky" Web pages*. Retrieved June 7, 2004, from http://webdesign.about.com/library/weekly/aa051500a.htm

Landow, G. P. (1994). *Hyper/text/theory*. Baltimore: Johns Hopkins University Press.

Landow, G. P. (1997). *Hypertext 2.0* (Rev. ed.). Baltimore: Johns Hopkins University Press.

Lanham, R. A. (1992). Digital rhetoric: Theory, practice, and property. In M. C. Tuman (Ed.), *Literacy online: The promise (and peril) of reading and writing with computers* (pp. 221–243). Pittsburgh, PA: University of Pittsburgh Press.

Lanham, R. A. (1993). *The electronic word: Democracy, technology, and the arts*. Chicago: University of Chicago Press.

Laurel, B. (1991). *Computers as theatre*. Reading, MA: Addison-Wesley.

Ledingham, J. A. (2000). Guidelines to building and maintaining strong organization-public relationship. *Public Relations Quarterly, 45*(3), 44–46.

Ledingham, J. A. (2003). Explicating relationship management as a general theory of public relations. *Journal of Public Relations Research, 15*(2), 181–198.

Ledingham, J. A. (2006). Relationship management: A general theory of public relations. In V. Hazleton & C. H. Botan (Eds.),

Public relations theory II (pp. 465–483). Mahwah, NJ: Lawrence Erlbaum Associates.

Ledingham, J. A., & Bruning, S. D. (1998). Relationship management in public relations: Dimensions of an organization-public relationship. *Public Relations Review, 24*(1), 55–65.

Ledingham, J. A., & Bruning, S. D. (1999). Time as an indicator of the perceptions and behavior of members of a key public: Monitoring and predicting organization-public relationships. *Journal of Public Relations Research, 11*(2), 167–183.

Ledingham, J. A., & Bruning, S. D. (2000). A longitudial study of organization-public relationship dimensions: Defining the role of communication in the practice of relationship management. In J. A. Ledingham & S. D. Bruning (Eds.), *Public relations as relationship management: A relational approach to the study and practice of public relations* (pp. 55–69). Mahwah, NJ: Lawrence Erlbaum Associates.

Lemke, J. L. (2002). Travels in hypermodality. *Visual communication, 1*(3), 299–325.

Len-Rios, M. L. (2003). *Communication rules and expectations in consumer use of information and e-commerce Web sites.* Paper presented at the International Communication Association Conference, San Diego, CA.

Lipinski, D., & Neddenriep, G. (2004). Using "new" media to get "old" media coverage. *The Harvard International Journal of Press/Politics, 9*(1), 7–21.

Lynch, P. J., & Horton, S. (2002). *Web style guide: Basic design principles for creating Web sites* (2nd ed.). New Haven, CT: Yale University Press.

Manovich, L. (2001). *The language of new media.* Cambridge, MA: MIT Press.

Marken, G. A. (2002). One-minute corporate reputation management (online public relations). *Public Relations Quarterly, 47*(4), 21–25.

Maynard, M., & Tian, Y. (2004). Between global and glocal: Content analysis of the Chinese Web Sites of the 100 top global brands. *Public Relations Review, 30*(3), 285–291.

McKeown, C. A., & Plowman, K. D. (1999). Reaching publics on the Web during the 1996 presidential campaign. *Journal of Public Relations Research, 11*(4), 321–347.

McMillan, S. J. (1999). Health communication and the Internet: Relations between interactive characteristics of the medium and site creators, content, and purpose. *Health Communication, 11*(4), 375–390.

McMillan, S. J. (2000). The microscope and the moving target: The challenge of applying content analysis to the World Wide Web. *Journalism and Mass Communication Quarterly, 77*(1), 80–98.

McPhee, S. (1997). Audio-visual poetics in interactive multimedia. *Convergence, 3*(4), 72–91.

Medco Health Solutions. (2004). *Medco Health Solutions corporate Web site.* Retrieved March 24, 2004, from http://www.medcohealth.com/medco/consumer/home.jsp

Mitra, A. (1997). Diasporic Web sites: Ingroup and outgroup discourse. *Critical Studies in Mass Communication, 14*(2), 158–181.

Moffet, J. (1998). *Washington journal: Internet server as an important tool in U.S. elections.* Retrieved March 25, 2003, from http://www.rferl.org/nca/features/1998/10/F.RU.981030103743.html

Mohammed, S. N. (2004). Self-presentation of small developing countries on the World Wide Web: A study of official Websites. *New Media & Society, 6*(4), 469–486.

Morkes, J., & Nielsen, J. (1997). *Concise, SCANNABLE, and objective: How to write for the Web.* Retrieved July 15, 2002, from http://www.useit.com/papers/webwriting/writing.html

Morville, P. (1996, February 23). Fixing Netscape. *Web Review.* Retrieved March 25, 2003, from http://semanticstudios.com/publications/web_architect/netscape.html

Naude, A. M. E., Froneman, J. D., & Atwood, R. A. (2004). The use of the Internet by ten South African non-governmental organizations—A public relations perspective. *Public Relations Review, 30*(1), 87–94.

Nelson, T. H. (1987). *Computer lib: Dream machines.* Redmond, WA: Microsoft Press.

Nelson, T. H. (1992). Opening hypertext: A memoir. In M. C. Tuman (Ed.), *Literacy online: The promise (and peril) of reading and writing with computers* (pp. 43–57). Pittsburgh, PA: University of Pittsburgh Press.

Neuman, W. L. (1991). *Social research methods: Qualitative and quantitative approaches.* Boston: Allyn and Bacon.

Newland Hill, L., & White, C. (2000). Public relations practitioners' perceptions of the World Wide Web as a communications tool. *Public Relations Review, 26*(1), 31–51.

Nielsen, J. (1993). *Usability engineering.* Boston: Academic Press.

Nielsen, J. (1997). *Loyalty on the Web.* Retrieved March 20, 2003, from www.useit.com/alertbox/9708a.html

Nielsen, J. (1999a). *"Top ten mistakes" revisited three years later.* Retrieved March 25, 2003, from http://www.useit.com/alertbox/990502.html

Nielsen, J. (1999b). *Usability as barrier to entry.* Retrieved June 8, 2004, from http://www.useit.com/alertbox/991128.html

Nielsen, J. (2000a). *Designing Web usability*. Indianapolis, IN: New Riders.

Nielsen, J. (2000b). *Drop-down menus: Use sparingly.* Retrieved June 4, 2004, from http://www.useit.com/alertbox/20001112.html

Nielsen, J. (2000c). *Eyetracking study of Web readers.* Retrieved March 25, 2003, from http://www.useit.com/alertbox/20000514.html

Nielsen, J. (2000d). *Is navigation useful?* Retrieved March 18, 2003, from www.useit.com/alertbox/20000109.html

Nielsen, J. (2000e). *Why you only need to test with 5 users.* Retrieved June 5, 2002, from http://www.useit.com/alertbox/20000319.html

Nielsen, J. (2001a). *Corporate Websites Get a 'D' in PR.* Retrieved May 20, 2004, from http://www.useit.com/alertbox/20010401.html

Nielsen, J. (2001b). *First rule of usability: Don't listen to users.* Retrieved January 10, 2003, from http://www.useit.com/alertbox/20010805.html

Nielsen, J. (2001c). *Tagline blues: What's the site about?* Retrieved March 21, 2003, from http://www.useit.com/alertbox/20010722.html

Nielsen, J. (2002). *User empowerment and the fun factor.* Retrieved March 25, 2003, from http://www.useit.com/alertbox/20020707.html

Nielsen, J. (2003a). *Investor relations Website design.* Retrieved March 25, 2003, from http://www.useit.com/alertbox/20030218.html

Nielsen, J. (2003b). *PR on Websites: Increasing usability.* Retrieved March 27, 2003, from http://www.useit.com/alertbox/20030310.html

Nielsen, J., & Loranger, H. (2006). *Prioritizing Web usability.* Berkeley, CA: New Riders.

Nielsen, J., & Norman, D. A. (2000). *Web-site usability: Usability on the Web isn't a luxury.* Retrieved March 24, 2003, from http://www.informationweek.com/773/web.htm

Nielsen, J., & Tahir, M. (2002). *Homepage usability: 50 Websites deconstructed.* Indianapolis, IN: New Riders.

Nielsen//NetRatings. (2003). *Global Internet population grows an average of four percent year-over-year.* Retrieved March 24, 2003, from http://www.nielsen-netratings.com/pr/pr_030220.pdf

Niven, D., & Zilber, J. (2001). Do women and men in Congress cultivate different images? Evidence from congressional Web sites. *Political Communication, 18*(4), 395–405.

North Coast Energy. (2004). *North Coast Energy corporate Web site.* Retrieved March 24, 2004, from http://www.northcoastenergy.com/

O'Leary, M. (2002). Not your father's Web site: Corporate sites emerge as new content innovators. *EContent, 25,* 20–24.

Packer, R., & Jordan, K. (2001). *Multimedia: From Wagner to virtual reality.* New York: Norton.

Papacharissi, Z. (2002). The presentation of self in virtual life: Characteristics of personal home pages. *Jornalism and Mass Communication Quarterly, 79*(3), 643–660.

Patton, M. Q. (2002). *Qualitative research & evaluation methods* (3rd ed.). Thousand Oaks, CA: Sage.

Paul, C. (2000). *When Web pages don't work: Steps you can take to improve the user experience on the Web.* Retrieved March 25, 2003, from http://www-106.ibm.com/developerworks/web/library/web-work.html

Perry, D. C., Taylor, M., & Doerfel, M. L. (2003). Internet-based communication in crisis management. *Management Communication Quarterly, 17*(2), 206–232.

Petty, R. E., & Cacioppo, J. T. (1981). *Attitudes and persuasion: Classic and contemporary approaches.* Dubuque, IA.

Pew Internet and American Life Project. (2002). *Use of the Internet at major life moments.* Retrieved June 27, 2002, from http://www.pewinternet.org/reports/toc.asp?Report=58

Pew Internet and American Life Project. (2003a). *Modest increase in Internet use for campaign 2002. Political sites gain, but major news sites still dominate.* Retrieved March 25, 2003, from http://www.pewinternet.org/reports/toc.asp?Report=82

Pew Internet and American Life Project. (2003b). *Untuned keyboards: Online campaigners, citizens, and portals in the 2002 elections.* Retrieved March 25, 2003, from http://www.pewinternet.org/reports/pdfs/PIP_IPDI_Politics_Report.pdf

Pew Internet and American Life Project. (2004). *How Americans get in touch with government.* Retrieved February 1, 2008, from http://www.pewinternet.org/PPF/r/128/report_display.asp

Pew Internet and American Life Project. (2005). *A decade of adoption: How the Internet has woven itself into American life.* Retrieved February 1, 2008, from http://www.pewinternet.org/PPF/r/148/report_display.asp

Pew Internet and American Life Project. (2007). *Election 2006 online.* Retrieved February 1, 2008, from http://www.pewinternet.org/PPF/r/199/report_display.asp

Pinterits, A., Treiblmaier, H., & Pollach, I. (2006). Environmental Websites: An empirical investigation of functionality and accessibility. *International Journal of Technology, Policy and Management, 6*(1), 103–119.

Powell, T. (2002). *Web design complete reference*. Berkeley, CA: McGraw-Hill Osborne Media.

Purcell, D., & Kodras, J. E. (2001). Information technologies and representational spaces at the outposts of the global political economy: Redrawing the Balkan image of Slovenia. *Information, Communication and Society, 4*(3), 341–369.

Rafaeli, S. (1988). Interactivity: From new media to communication. In R. P. Hawkins, J. M. Wiemann, & S. Pingree (Eds.), *Advancing communication science: Merging mass and interpersonal processes* (pp. 110–134). Newbury Park, CA: Sage.

Randall, N. (1997). *The soul of the Internet: Net gods, netizens and the wiring of the world*. Boston: International Thomson Computer Press.

Reavy, M., & Perlmutter, D. D. (1997). Presidential Web sites as sources of information [Electronic version]. *Electronic Journal of Communication, 7*(3). Retrieved March 21, 2003 from http://www.cios.org/getfile/Reavy_V7N397

Reber, B. H., & Kim, J. K. (2006). How activist groups use Websites in media relations: Evaluating online press rooms. *Journal of Public Relations Research, 18*(4), 313–333.

Reinard, J. C. (1994). *Introduction to communication research*. Madison, WI: Brown and Benchmark.

Robbins, S. S., & Stylianou, A. C. (2003). Global corporate Web sites: An empirical investigation of content and design. *Information and Management, 40*(3), 205–212.

Russell, M. C. (2002). *Fortune 500 revisited: Current trends in sitemap design*. Retrieved March 21, 2003, from http://wsupsy.psy.twsu.edu/surl/usabilitynews/42/sitemaps.htm

Sandman, P. M. (1993). *Responding to community outrage: Strategies for effective risk communication.* Fairfax, VA: American Industrial Hygiene Association.

Scruton, R. (2001). *Kant: A very short introduction.* New York: Oxford University Press.

Segaller, S. (1999). *Nerds 2.0.1: A brief history of the Internet.* New York: TV Books.

Shedroff, N. (2001). *Experience design.* Indianapolis, IN: New Riders.

Sims, R. (1997). Interactivity: A forgotten art? *Computers in Human Behavior, 13*(2), 157–180.

Slatin, J. M. (1991). Composing hypertext: A discussion for writing teachers. In E. Berk & J. Devlin (Eds.), *Hypertext/hypermedia handbook* (pp. 55–64). New York: McGraw Hill.

Smith, M. J. (1988). *Contemporary communication research methods.* Belmont, CA: Wadsworth.

Soukup, C. (2000). Building a theory of multi-media CMC. *New Media & Society, 2*(4), 407–425.

Souza, R., Manning, H., Sonderegger, P., Roshan, S., & Dorsey, M. (2001). *Get ROI from design.* Retrieved July 21, 2002, from http://www.uk.cgey.com/services/crm/docs/roi__design.pdf

Spool, J. M. (1999). *Web site usability: A designer's guide.* San Francisco: Morgan Kaufmann Publishers.

Stewart, W. (2002). *How the Net was invented.* Retrieved July 16, 2002, from http://livinginternet.com/

Taylor, M., & Kent, M. L. (2004). Congressional Web sites and their potential for public dialogue. *Atlantic Journal of Communication, 12*(2), 59–76.

Taylor, M., Kent, M. L., & White, W. J. (2001). How activist organizations are using the Internet to build relationships. *Public Relations Review, 27*(3), 263–284.

Tian, Y. (2006). Communicating with local publics: A case study of Coca-Cola's Chinese Web site. *Corporate Communications: An International Journal, 11*(1), 13–22.

U.S. Department of Commerce. (2002). *A nation online: How Americans are expanding their use of the Internet.* Retrieved December 12, 2002, from http://www.ntia.doc.gov/ntiahome/dn/

U.S. Department of Commerce. (2004). *A nation online: Entering the Broadband Age.* Retrieved February 1, 2008, from http:// www.ntia.doc.gov/reports/anol/NationOnlineBroadband04. htm

Valero Energy. (2004). *Valero Energy corporate Web site.* Retrieved March 14, 2004, from http://www.valero.com/

Van Duyne, D. K., Landay, J. A., & Hong, J. I. (2003). *The design of sites: Patterns, principles, and processes for crafting a customer-centered Web experience.* Reading, MA: Addison-Wesley.

Vasquez, G. M. (1993). A homo narrans paradigm for public relations: Combining Bormann's symbolic convergence theory and Grunig's situational theory of publics. *Journal of Public Relations Research, 5*(3), 201–216.

Virbac. (2004). *Virbac corporate Web site.* Retrieved March 24, 2004, from http://www.virbaccorp.com/

Westcorp. (2004). *Westcorp corporate Web site.* Retrieved March 24, 2004, from http://www.westcorpinc.com/

Weyerhaeuser. (2004). *Weyerhaeuser corporate Web site.* Retrieved March 24, 2004, from http://www.weyerhaeuser.com/

White, C., & Raman, N. (2000). The World Wide Web as a public relations medium: The use of research, planning, and evaluation in Web site development. *Public Relations Review, 25*(4), 405–419.

Whitman, J. R. (2004). *The meaningful power of the 10-point scale*. Retrieved March 15, 2004, from http://www.surveytools.com/scale.htm

Wilde, E. (1999). *Wilde's WWW: Technical foundations of the World Wide Web*. New York: Springer Verlag.

Will, E. M., & Callison, C. (2006). Web presence of universities: Is higher education sending the right message? *Public Relations Review, 32*(2), 180–183.

Will, M., & Porak, V. (2000). Corporate communication in the new media environment. A survey of 150 corporate communication Web sites [Electronic version]. *International Journal of Media Management, 2*. Retrieved July 21, 2002, from http://www.mediamanagement.org/modules/pub/view.php/mediajournal-44

Wood, A. F., & Smith, M. J. (2001). *Online communication: Linking technology, identity, and culture*. Mahwah, NJ: Lawrence Erlbaum Associates.

Zhang, J., & Benoit, W. L. (2004). Message strategies of Saudi Arabia's image restoration campaign after 9/11. *Public Relations Review, 30*(2), 161–167.

INDEX